D0773017

Trollope in the Post Office

Trollope in the Post Office

R. H. SUPER

Ann Arbor
The University of Michigan Press

Library of Congress Cataloging in Publication Data

Super, R. H. (Robert Henry), 1914–
  Trollope in the Post Office.

  Includes bibliographical references and index.
  1. Trollope, Anthony, 1815–1882—Biography—
Careers.   2.   Novelists, English—19th century—
Biography.   3.   Postal service—Great Britain—
Employees—Biography.   4.   Postal service—Great
Britain—History.   5.   Great Britain. Post Office.
I. Title.
PR5686.S9 1981   823'.8 [B]   81-10363
ISBN 0-472-10013-0   AACR2

For Willard Thorp
Who half a century ago introduced me to Trollope

Preface

The General Post Office in St. Martin's-le-Grand in which Trollope spent a large part of his working life was demolished in 1913; of the three nineteenth-century buildings that made up the Post Office complex only one, the North Building, still stands, and that was built after Trollope's death. It is a quiet building, with a touch of ancient grandeur, and in the basement is housed the Records Department, with a small but busy staff and a room for researchers. The staff—whose names I'm sorry to say I never learned—were unobtrusive but had a way of turning up the information one needed, precisely when needed. In general they believed in letting one learn by observation how matters were arranged instead of explaining them unnecessarily. Researchers were for the most part stamp collectors or students of postmarks and local postal histories; there were no other historians of literature. But they too were helpful; one of them was quick to diagram for me the makeup of a sheet of postage stamps in the reign of Queen Victoria in answer to a question I asked him, and in so doing made clear a rather amusing game Trollope played with his readers in *John Caldigate*. I cannot claim to have turned up every trace of Trollope in the records—far from it—but believe I have found the most important of the surviving documents and from them have constructed the principal outlines of the accompanying story.

In *An Autobiography* Trollope professes to give an account of himself as a writer, but there is a great deal in it also of his Post Office experience, and his dedication to the Civil Service shows up almost as strongly as his dedication to fiction. The work has so completely dominated his biographers that they have seldom looked very energetically beyond it for their materials. In the present little book, *An Autobiography* has been thrust into the background; occasionally I have used it to embellish my tale, but by no means every story Trollope tells us there about his career has been repeated in these pages. He was a great keeper of records in his own right and had his records with him when he wrote, yet even his dates were occasionally wrong and certainly his memory for details was at times finely fictive. It has seemed pointless to conduct a running debate with him. When my account differs from his, it may be assumed that the weight of the evidence is against his version—the evidence of documents, of letters, of contemporary narratives. He will be found to be not seriously discredited, but some emphases will have changed.

This is the story of a civil servant who was also a novelist, and who consciously drew upon his own experiences in the writing of his fictions. No small part of the aim of this book is to show the connection between the two aspects of his life. "In England, as in Ireland, it was the Post Office servant who made the novelist," said his first biographer.

In addition to expressing my gratitude to the Post Office Records Department, I should like to thank the curators of the Parrish Collection at Princeton University for making available the traveling journals Trollope

kept as a Post Office official and those of the Beinecke
Rare Book and Manuscript Library at Yale University
for responding to my questions about the manuscript of
Phineas Finn. Mr. Scott Bennett and Ms. Mary Ceibert
were most hospitable during my visit to the Rare Book
Room of the University of Illinois Library. For Trollope's dates at Harrow I am indebted to Mr. J. S. Gol-
land, at Winchester to Mr. Roger Custance. My thanks
are also due to Professor N. John Hall for giving me in
advance the copy for his forthcoming edition of Trollope's correspondence (Stanford University Press) and
to my friend and colleague Professor James Gindin and
my student Ms. Judith Wittosch Kelley for their close
and helpful reading of the manuscript. Professor Ruth
apRoberts and another well-informed scholar whose
name has not been revealed to me read the manuscript
on behalf of my publisher and made suggestions that
have much improved the work. The research for the
book was done during my tenure of a fellowship from
the National Endowment for the Humanities.

Contents

Trollope in the Post Office

The Post Office Appointment

In 1834 Trollope was nineteen years old. His schooling had been cut off when he was in the sixth form (the top level) and a monitor at Harrow school: his father's financial failure had taken the family in haste to Bruges, and Anthony was serving temporarily as a junior instructor in an English school at Brussels conducted by a member of the numerous Harrow family of Drury, while he sought some permanent career.[1] Back in London, one of his mother's dearest friends was married to Clayton Freeling, a civil servant and son of Sir Francis Freeling, secretary to the Post Office. It was but natural that she should involve herself in the search for a position for Anthony. (The Freelings were from Bristol, as was Frances Trollope's father.) About the middle of October, 1834, young Frederick Diggle, after an unsatisfactory career of some two and a half years as junior clerk in the office of the secretary, was permitted to resign from the Post Office in order to avoid dismissal. On the twenty-eighth, Anthony's brother Tom learned in London that G. H. Freeling, Clayton's older brother and assistant secretary, was prepared to offer the vacant position to Anthony. On November 4, the appointment was routinely approved by the postmaster general. "Mr. Trollope has been well educated and will be subject to the usual probation as to competency," wrote Sir Francis.[2] There was no civil service examination in those days: Trollope was asked to demonstrate the legibility of his handwriting and when he failed miserably in the demonstration was told to copy a passage carefully at home and bring it back with him next day. He was never asked to show it, and a threatened examination in arithmetic never took place. Twenty-six years later Trollope told a large audience of Post Office employees and their families that the Civil Service was a profession young men seldom chose; it was chosen for them by impecunious parents "because an early income was desirable."[3]

Handwriting was indeed the one accomplishment a junior clerk needed: day after day he was set to work copying—copying letters into the letter book, minutes into the minute book. It was no doubt to be hoped that by copying the correspondence the brighter clerks would learn the business. For the rest, punctuality and attentiveness to the work were desirable, but not always achieved. Trollope's salary would be £90 a year for the first three years, then would rise to £110; there were further increases after seven and ten years, but by that time one would have been either promoted or dismissed. (The scale was raised two years later to £110 and £140.)[4] Of the seven junior clerks in the room with Trollope, several rose (as he did) to surveyorships and ended their careers in those posts of responsibility; one, John Tilley, five years senior to Trollope in the service, in due course (thirty years later) became secretary, the highest permanent officer in the Post Office.[5] Their place of work was the magnificent new Post Office building in St. Martin's-le-Grand (demolished 1913).

Sir Francis Freeling's secretaryship went back to the last decade of the previous century; he soon became too ill to perform his duties regularly, and he died a little more than a year and a half after Trollope's appointment. He was succeeded by Lt. Col. William Leader

Maberly, who was something of a martinet; Trollope's description of him suggests that the two were in constant conflict, but the slight evidence of the records suggests that he was on the whole well disposed to Trollope. He was commissioned lieutenant in the army a few months before Waterloo and rose to his present rank before going on half pay in 1832. He had married an Irish heiress, and according to Edmund Yates his principal concerns were his Irish incomes and his wife's extravagance. Incidentally, he lived long enough to have read what was said about him in Trollope's *Autobiography*.[6] Sir Boreas Bodkin, nicknamed Aeolus ("Windbag"), in *Marion Fay* (1882) is somewhat modeled on him—"a violent and imperious Secretary, but not in the main ill-natured" (chap. 7).

Instructions in the office were given in writing, and each junior was obliged to acknowledge his awareness of them by signing in the margin.[7] A glorious "Anthony Trollope" heads the list of signatures acknowledging the order to use the hour from ten to eleven to enter minutes in the minute books and index the books, instead of eating breakfast. The work did not proceed as it should have done, and two months later Trollope and his fellows had to acknowledge that unless they caught up with the work they would be obliged to remain after four o'clock to get it done. (The normal working day was from ten to four.) Several chapters of *Marion Fay* are set in the clerks' room as Trollope remembered it.

Though the records give us little information about his conduct in his earliest years, the evidence of the minute books from 1838 onward makes him look most unpromising.[8] Shortly before Christmas, he failed to copy and dispatch some important letters about postal arrangements to the railway companies, and his superior, the assistant secretary, was by no means satisfied with his explanation. "I have observed with much regret an habitual carelessness on the part of this Officer, in the performance of his duties." And so he was suspended from pay for a week and most seriously warned by the postmaster general "that unless there is a great alteration in his attention to his duties, I shall be under the necessity of removing him from the service." In April, 1839, he overstayed a weekend leave by half a day and was threatened with another suspension of pay, but on this occasion seems to have offered a good explanation. The next month, however, he was found to have fallen so far behind in his work through tardiness that he was compelled to make up the time after hours, and was seriously penalized by the loss of the seniority which would have entitled him to the next promotion. "I regret to be compelled to make such a proposition but Mr. Trollope is without excuse, as he has good abilities & as this neglect, which has undoubtedly brought the Dept. into discredit (for some of the Cases are most gross) is entirely produced by the want of proper attention to his duty," wrote Maberly. In November, 1840, the junior clerks to a man were found remiss about following instructions for reporting expenditures to the accountant general, but Trollope was especially remiss.[9] Despite these memoranda, Trollope (at least when he grew older) remembered the discipline of the office as incredibly lax. He told the story of one junior clerk called before his superior and confronted with copies of letters he had entered in the minute book the preceding day. "If you can read *one line* of this, I shan't dismiss you," said the superior. Alas, the unfortunate lad could not— he had merely scrawled on the page in pretense of copying, and so he was dismissed.[10] The implication that such delinquents often escaped detection is not borne out by the minute books I have seen, which are relatively legible and in good order.

In February, 1841, an Irish £3 bank note was found improperly enclosed in a newspaper in the post, and was given to Trollope to deal with. When, in due course, the money was unclaimed it became the property of the Revenue, but it was then discovered that Trollope had not used the proper procedure for recording the note and it had disappeared. He was at first required "to make good the loss occasioned by his carelessness & neglect of regulations," but again he had an explanation—a statement of what he had conceived to have been the correct procedure in such a case; he was wrong, said his superiors, but he was not made to pay up.[11] One wonders if this was the simple foundation of a story he told in *An Autobiography:*

> On one occasion, in the performance of my duty, I had put a private letter containing bank-notes on the Secretary's table,—which letter I had duly opened, as it was not marked private. The letter was seen by the Colonel, but had not been moved by him when he left his room. On his return it was gone. In the meantime I had returned to the room, again in the performance of some duty. When the letter was missed I was sent for, and there I found the Colonel much moved about his letter, and a certain chief clerk, who, with a long face, was making suggestions as to the probable fate of the money. "The letter has been taken," said the Colonel, turning to me angrily, "and, by G——! there has been nobody in the room but you and I." As he spoke, he thundered his fist down upon the table. "Then," said I, "by G——! you have taken it." And I also thundered my fist down;—but, accidentally, not upon the table. There was there a standing movable desk, at which, I presume, it was the Colonel's habit to write, and on this movable desk was a large bottle full of ink. My fist unfortunately came on the desk, and the ink at once flew up, covering the Colonel's face and shirt-front.

Then it was a sight to see that senior clerk, as he seized a quire of blotting-paper, and rushed to the aid of his superior officer, striving to mop up the ink; and a sight also to see the Colonel, in his agony, hit right out through the blotting-paper at that senior clerk's unoffending stomach. At that moment there came in the Colonel's private secretary, with the letter and the money, and I was desired to go back to my own room. This was an incident not much in my favour, though I do not know that it did me special harm.[12]

Many years later (1880) Trollope defended Cicero for saying that a speaker must from time to time make use of "little tiny lies." "The advice does not indeed refer to facts, or to evidence, or to arguments. It goes no further than to suggest that amount of exaggeration which is used by every teller of a good story in order that the story may be good. Such 'mendaciuncula' are in the mouth of every diner-out in London and we may pity the dinner parties at which they are not used."[13] Of course the Post Office minutes may be describing a more prosaic dispute over lost currency than the incident described in *An Autobiography*, but the reader of that book often delights in what he nevertheless may prudently suspect to be a Trollopian *mendaciunculum*.

There is today in the General Post Office in London precisely the kind of movable desk Trollope mentions, a sort of low, portable, desk-top lectern which now at any rate is shown as having been the one at which he himself worked. And it was perhaps a recollection of the breach of postal regulations involved in the attempted transmission of the Irish bank note that led him to ask, in *Brown, Jones, and Robinson*, "Who can make a widow understand that she should not communicate with her boy in the colonies under the dishonest cover of a newspaper?" (chap. 14).

At first he and Tom lived together in lodgings kept

by a tailor and his mother on Little Marlborough
Street, just off Regent Street close to Oxford Circus;
Phineas Finn lived in lodgings near there as a young
law student just arrived in London. Anthony's brother
described the lodgings as

> a queer house, disconnected with the row of buildings
> in which it stood, a survival of some earlier period. It
> stood in its own court, by which it was separated from
> the street. . . . The lodgings were very cheap, more so I
> think than the goodness of them might have justified.
> We were the only lodgers; and the cheapness of the
> rooms was, I suspect, in some degree caused by the fact
> that the majority of young men lodgers would not have
> tolerated the despotic rule of our old landlady, the tai-
> lor's mother. She made us very comfortable; but her
> laws were many [and inflexible].[14]

Tom did not remain long in London after Anthony's
arrival, and Anthony then took solitary lodgings on
Northumberland Street, Marylebone (now Luxborough
Street), in a room looking out on the back door of the
Marylebone Workhouse across the way (where the new
buildings of the London Polytechnic now stand). Mrs.
Trollope had stayed there briefly with her children
Henry and Emily in September of 1834. It was from
this house that the wretched Mr. Emilius slipped out
to murder Bonteen in *Phineas Redux*. Trollope later regarded these early years in London as the most lonely
and miserable of his life, even though on his testimony
he did have friends with whom he went on outings in
the country. He was alone in lodgings, alone in finding
his dinners in restaurants; breakfasts his landlady
might prepare for him on credit, but the dinners required cash. Reading was possible to pass the time, and
Trollope attempted an ambitious program of
reading—but there are limits to the reading a lonely

and restless young man can tolerate. His mother sought through her publisher, John Murray, to secure for him after-hours employment as a corrector of the press, or something of the kind. There was no kinsman near except his mother's brother Henry Milton, a clerk in the War Office, and he lived in a remote part of town. Sociability was to be found with the other clerks at the Post Office itself (about three miles from his lodgings), but that was much too close to the eye of his superiors, who were not reluctant to criticize his inattention to duty, and a group of equally lonely young men might not always be discreet in their mode of seeking recreation.[15] A good many years later, close to his retirement, he remarked (when discussing the Civil Service Commission's concern for the moral character of those to whom it granted its certificates):

> Many a young clerk became bad in character under the auspices of the Service. Many a lad placed alone in London, with six hours' work to be done in the day and with no amusements provided for his evenings, has gone to shivers on the rocks of Metropolitan life. Many more will continue to do so till parents confess the necessity of providing recreation as well as that of providing work. But these have been evils that have come subsequent to the appointment, and could have been prevented by no previous inquiries. Nor have such evils been in any degree mitigated by the doings of the Commissioners.[16]

At the beginning of 1837 Mrs. Trollope took a house in the suburban village of Hadley, north of London; there, within a few weeks, her daughter Emily died of tuberculosis. (Trollope describes her burial in Hadley churchyard in *The Bertrams* [1859, vol. 2, chap. 15].) Anthony was a frequent visitor there, occasionally accompanied by his fellow clerk John Tilley, who thus met his future wife Cecilia Trollope. The episode is paralleled in *Marion Fay,* where Lord Hampstead brings to his

home in Hendon, not far from Hadley, a young Post
Office clerk who thus meets Hampstead's sister and in
time becomes *her* husband. In the late autumn of 1838
Mrs. Trollope and Cecilia moved to Number 20, York
Street, Marylebone, not far from Northumberland
Street, and both Tom and Anthony lived with them
there. Life was for a time more comfortable and more
economical, but Mrs. Trollope was as restless as ever,
and before long Anthony was once more left alone. His
serious illness of the late spring and summer of 1840,
for which his mother returned from Paris to nurse him
and during which his life was feared for, is recorded in
the Post Office minute book of May and June.[17] The
experiences of *The Three Clerks* and of Johnny Eames in
The Small House at Allington are somewhat transformed
from Trollope's memories of this part of his life.

The Move to Ireland

The way upward in the postal service from a
clerkship in the secretary's office was through
the surveyorships, or (one might call them)
district superintendencies of the mails. The surveyor
was responsible for every aspect of the postal service in
his district, including the supervision of deliveries and
of postmasters, looking into complaints and suggesting
improvements. And the normal path to a surveyorship
was to become a surveyor's clerk, or assistant. The position obviously gave valuable insight into the workings of
the system, and at a time when railways were expanding
rapidly the surveyors had a sense that they were break-
ing important new ground. In 1838 John Tilley, who
had reached the maximum salary of £180 per annum as

a junior clerk, was appointed surveyor for the Northern District of England at a salary of £300. On February 11, 1839, before he took up his new post, he married Cecilia Trollope at St. Mary's Church, Bryanston Square; the ceremony was performed by the bibliophile T. F. Dibdin in the presence of a large group of witnesses that of course included the bride's mother and brothers, the Milton cousins, and at least one other young official from the Post Office.[18]

Some two years later, word came of a vacancy for a surveyor's clerk in the Central District of Ireland. The information crossed Trollope's desk first, and he perceived a way out of the unmitigated dreariness and sense of failure in his London office: he requested the transfer and was appointed on July 29, 1841. *An Autobiography* makes it appear that the move to Ireland was regarded in London as a most undesirable one and that Colonel Maberly, who rejoiced to be rid of him, could hardly believe that Trollope wanted to go. Nevertheless, three of the surveyors' clerks in Ireland at about this time were named Maberly.[19]

Trollope was granted a fortnight's leave from the beginning of September, preparatory to the move. But his departure from the secretary's office was not without a storm. He quarreled with a fellow clerk named Adolphus Shelley (not of the poet's family), used violent and insulting language, and was reported to the postmaster general, who (on Maberly's suggestion) required him to write a letter of apology to Shelley; "any refusal on his part to give it will be at his peril." Trollope complied.[20]

He borrowed £200 from "a dear old cousin, our family lawyer," to secure his release from his London debts and pay his way to Ireland. The cousin "looked upon me with pitying eyes,—shaking his head," for Ireland was a place of last resort to an Englishman. But the money was repaid a few years later and the cousin gently admitted that after all Anthony had been right to go. On September 15, he landed in Dublin, spent the night at a dirty hotel, and (by way of fitting himself into the supposed character of his new countrymen) ordered some whiskey punch after dinner. It was a brave gesture that did little to remove his loneliness. Next morning he called on the secretary of the Irish Post Office and learned that Maberly had sent a letter of warning that the young man was thoroughly unreliable; "but I shall judge you by your own merits," the secretary said. (There is no record of such a letter in the Post Office files.) On the nineteenth he reached Banagher, a town on the River Shannon almost exactly in the center of Ireland, and headquarters of the Central District.[21]

The surveyor of the district since 1833 had been the somewhat cantankerous James Drought. (It was doubtless one of his relatives, the stodgy Sir Orlando Drought, who, offended by the Duke of Omnium's inattention to him, caused the downfall of Omnium's government in *The Prime Minister*.) Central Ireland was the least desirable of the Irish districts, and in making the move Trollope also took a reduction in salary from the £180 a year he would have received at his former post to £100, but to the new salary were added travel allowances of fifteen shillings for every day spent away from his base and sixpence a mile for conveyance; the prudent management of his arrangements would let him more than triple his salary. He was therefore obliged to keep a careful record of his movements, and the notebooks in which he kept this record survive. "Do not be too economical," he advised a young surveyor's clerk more than a decade later. "You should always live at the hotels as a gentleman. It will pay best in the long run." The allowances were at the same rate in England and Ireland, but travel in the latter country cost only about half as much and so one could put a great deal more into one's pocket. In *An Autobiography* he says that his income after expenses became at once £400; that is a slight exaggeration.[22]

Trollope speaks with some pride of the speed with which he learned his task. The postmaster of Oranmore had been suspected of being behind in his accounts; the new clerk first made the man show him how the accounts were required to be kept, then found him to owe a substantial amount and recommended that he be dismissed as an incorrigible defaulter. Dismissed he was on November 1 and later was found to have been even further in arrears than at first supposed.[23] Not all was triumph, however. The secretary in London disallowed Trollope's claim for reimbursement of the cost of his travel from London to Dublin, and a month after his arrival the decision that he must pay back the missing £3 note reached him. The penalty, to be sure, was later revoked.[24]

Here at Banagher he found that the surveyor kept a pack of hounds; the expenses of living in Ireland were so much less than they had been in London that he quickly bought himself a horse, learned to ride to the hounds, and found for himself one of his principal leisure occupations for more than forty years.[25]

Engagement and Marriage

 Trollope was on duty from July 9 to August 2, 1842, at the seaside resort of Kingstown, outside Dublin. There he made the acquaintance of Edward Heseltine, Rotherham agent of the Sheffield and Rotherham Banking Company, and his wife and daughters. Possibly the introduction came about through a young clerk from the Inland Office of the Post Office in London, Thomas Bland, who not long afterward was transferred to the Irish establishment as a surveyor's clerk: one of Heseltine's daughters was married to a Joseph Bland, clerk in the Rotherham bank.[26] Rotherham was a market town of about 8,000 inhabitants six miles distant from Sheffield, which then had a population of over 110,000; it shared some of Sheffield's industry but still had strong contacts with the country and had also a strong sense of its own identity. Its church dated from the reign of Edward IV (fifteenth century). The bank offices were in an imposing old house on the High Street, and the manager and his family lived above them; legend had it that both Mary Queen of Scots and Charles I had stayed the night in that house when traveling as prisoners toward London. One of Heseltine's junior clerks many years later recalled how the manager sunned himself daily on fine days, "with his blue coat and gilt buttons, a chevalier of the old school." ("Another antique figure was the Earl of Effingham, [with his] flesh coloured pantaloons, shoes, and buckles"; Trollope borrowed the name for one of his more attractive heroines.) Heseltine was, as befitted his position, one of the town's leading citizens and a director of the Sheffield and Rotherham Railway, opened in 1838. He had a hobby of collecting armor.[27]

Clearly Kingstown was attractive. Trollope returned there for a fortnight's holiday in mid-August, then quickly applied for a two-week extension of his leave and it was granted. Heseltine's fourth daughter, Rose, and he seemed to know at once that they were meant for each other. Trollope's proposal scenes in his novels follow a pattern of convention that is hardly credible to the modern reader: "Say it shall be so," says the hero, and the heroine acknowledges that it shall be so—or she does not. Trollope admitted the difficulty facing the novelist who must describe an event he may only once have participated in and never otherwise observed. Nevertheless,

the absolute words and acts of one such scene did once come to the author's knowledge. The couple were by no means plebeian, or below the proper standard of high bearing and high breeding; they were a handsome pair, living among educated people, sufficiently given to mental pursuits, and in every way what a pair of polite lovers ought to be. The all-important conversation passed in this wise. The site of the passionate scene was the seashore, on which they were walking, in autumn.

Gentleman. "Well, Miss ———, the long and the short of it is this: here I am; you can take me or leave me."

Lady—scratching a gutter on the sand with her parasol, so as to allow a little salt water to run out of one hole into another. "Of course, I know that's all nonsense."

Gentleman. "Nonsense! By Jove, it isn't nonsense at all: come, Jane; here I am: come, at any rate you can say something."

Lady. "Yes, I suppose I can say something."

Gentleman. "Well, which is it to be; take me or leave me?"

Lady—very slowly, and with a voice perhaps hardly articulate, carrying on, at the same time, her engineering works on a wider scale. "Well, I don't exactly want to leave you."

And so the matter was settled: settled with much propriety and satisfaction; and both the lady and gentleman would have thought, had they ever thought about the matter at all, that this, the sweetest moment of their lives, had been graced by all the poetry by which such moments ought to be hallowed.[28]

It was another two years before Trollope's salary rose to a point that would permit the couple to be married. Trollope throughout his career firmly believed that promotion in the Civil Service (at least through the ordinary ranks) should be based strictly on seniority; a person had a right to know what he could count on for the future—had a right, as Trollope told his superiors many years later, to plan such an important step as marriage with some assurance of his future progress in the service. The couple were married at the parish church in Rotherham on Tuesday, June 11, 1844; the newspapers described the groom as "son of the celebrated authoress." In the margin of his travel account book Trollope wrote simply, near this date, "married." Rose, jotting down her recollections of the events of their life at the end of 1875, presumably to assist him in his work on *An Autobiography*, began the account with: "1844. Married 11th June. (hurrah)." Her introduction to Banagher on August 2 was enlivened by their being inadvertently driven into the Shannon canal by the driver of the cart that conveyed them.

Trollope's was not an occupation that made marriage easy. Occasionally he was able to settle in one place (with Rose) for a period—at Cork for September–February, 1844–45; then in temporary charge of the post offices at Milltown Malbay on the west coast from March to mid-June, 1845; at Kilkenny in October; and at Fermoy for most of November–February, 1845–46—but there was also much traveling: from May 9 to September 21, 1846, for example, a few weeks after the birth of his first son, he was in a different town nearly every night.[29]

It is not unlikely that Trollope made some firsthand acquaintance with the West Riding and Nottinghamshire hunts when he visited Rotherham. One of them was the Rufford Hunt, and one of the points of rendezvous for another of the local hunts was Scrooby Inn; readers of *The American Senator* will find both names familiar.

The year before his marriage, while temporarily stationed at the little town of Drumsna on the River Shannon in county Leitrim, Trollope and his old friend John Merivale, who was visiting him, came upon an abandoned mansion in the course of one of their country walks. They speculated why it should have become derelict, and Trollope framed from their speculations the plot of his first novel, *The Macdermots of Ballycloran*, which he began to write in September, 1843, as soon as Merivale departed. He had long had the notion of becoming a novelist, but (unlike the work of his later career) progress upon this book was slow. Only a third of it was written by the date of his marriage; a year later (July, 1845) it was finished and it was published about the middle of March, 1847.[30]

Trollope in Ireland

Trollope remained in the Central District of Ireland only until August 27, 1844, when, having failed to secure a transfer to the Northern District as his first choice, he was sent to the Southern District as clerk to the surveyor there, James Kendrick, who remained his superior until he secured his own district. Thomas Bland replaced him in the Central District.[31] His headquarters were thenceforward at Clonmel, in Tipperary, where he took lodgings

and where his sons Henry Merivale and Frederic James
Anthony were born (March 13, 1846, and September
27, 1847); Frederic was the name of Rose's younger
brother. Henry's godparents were John Lewis Merivale, his uncle Thomas Adolphus, and his grand-
mother Frances Trollope; Fred's were James Kendrick,
John Tilley, and Isabella Heseltine.[32] Clonmel was a
town of some size on the Suir, with some fine old buildings, and was a famous sporting center, the headquarters of the Tipperary foxhounds. When the Irish
districts were redivided to provide a fourth surveyor in
February, 1848, Trollope at first requested and was
granted a transfer that would permit him to remain in
Clonmel (now made a part of the South Midland District), but he remained with Kendrick when both were
permitted to retain their headquarters there until they
could at their leisure dispose of their houses and move
their families. Late in the year the Trollopes moved to
Mallow, in county Cork, where they took a house and
where the hunting was, if anything, even better.[33] Just
as *The Kellys and the O'Kellys* was largely set in Trollope's
first district, so *Castle Richmond* takes place chiefly in his
new one in county Cork.

In December, 1848, Maberly was obliged to draw the
attention of the postmaster general to a quarrel Trollope got himself involved in with a mail guard named
Conolly, whom Trollope tried to bar from the post office at Fermoy: there was an explosion of some magni-
tude between the men and each made written accusations against the other. Maberly tried to temporize by
cautioning Conolly that superior officers must on all
occasions be treated "with becoming deference & respect," and by warning Trollope to be careful in his
conduct toward his inferiors so as "not to give rise to

these unpleasant charges against him." Trollope was im-
prudent enough to remonstrate against the warning and
was told bluntly that in the secretary's view he had been
quite simply wrong in his conduct toward Conolly.[34]

It is always gratifying to foil a cheat by superior wit.
One of Anthony's anecdotes is related by Tom Trollope, who heard from his brother so many stories of his
official experiences that he felt himself competent to
write a book of "Memoirs of a Post Office Surveyor"
(though he never did so). Again, it was a tale of a
dishonest postmaster in the southwest of Ireland. On a
visit of inspection Trollope had noticed that the man
carefully locked a large desk in the office. Two eve-
nings later, word reached Trollope that a letter of some
value was missing; the man's behavior had been suspicious, and so on the instant Trollope hired a horse and
rode to the distant office. Rousing the postmaster in
the small hours, he strode into the office and de-
manded that the desk be opened. Unfortunately, said
the postmaster, the key had been lost for some months.
And so Trollope kicked open the desk and (of course)
found the missing letter. Cicero would have approved
of the story.[35] A parallel tale is confirmed by the newspapers of the day. In 1848 complaints came in of letters and cash lost from the mails that passed through
Tralee, and so Trollope wrote a letter from a fictitious
father in Newcastle (Limerick) enclosing a marked sovereign to a fictitious daughter in Ardfert, had it sealed
in the bag at Newcastle on September 18, then sped to
Ardfert to await its arrival. The bag had to be opened
at Tralee as a distributing center, and the letters con-
signed to other bags; when the proper bag reached
Ardfert Trollope's letter was not in it. And so he hastened to Tralee, where, accompanied by a constable

with a search warrant, he found the marked sovereign
in the purse of Mary O'Reilly, assistant to the postmaster. As a witness at her trial on July 26, 1849, Trollope was subjected to cross-examination by the future
leader of the Home Rule party in the House of Commons, Isaac Butt, who turned the questioning into a
silly debate with Trollope about the location of the
mark he had placed on the coin—"under the neck on
the head" (i.e., on the obverse side of the coin); "under
the neck on the head" is anatomically impossible, said
Butt, and the two wrangled in high good humor. Butt
called attention to Trollope's reflections on Irish judges
and barristers (Allewinde and O'Laugher) in *The Macdermots of Ballycloran*. Perhaps this episode may be seen
as an anticipation of Chaffanbrass's cross-examination
of the novelist Bouncer at the trial of Phineas Finn
(*Phineas Redux* [1873], chap. 61); it was certainly behind
Trollope's description of the liveliness of the Irish as-
sizes in *Castle Richmond* (chap. 35).[36]

On a visit to London Trollope presented himself to
John Forster, editor of the Liberal weekly newspaper
the *Examiner,* with the offer of a series of letters on the
government's measures in relief of the disasters of the
potato famine and the pestilence—a subject about
which he had some claim to knowledge from his constant travels about the country; the consequence of this
offer was the publication in the *Examiner* of seven letters on the state of Ireland in 1849–50. A decade later
the Ireland of the famine was the subject of his novel
Castle Richmond. He also volunteered to write a handbook to Ireland for the series of guides brought out by
John Murray, one of Mrs. Trollope's publishers, but
this venture came to nothing when Murray neglected
to open the parcel containing a substantial sample of

the work, and finally after a delay of nine months returned it, still unopened, in response to an angry letter
from the author.[37]

Reorganizing Rural Posts

Rowland Hill in 1840 effected the establishment of the penny post (and invented the
adhesive postage stamp) as an officer of the
Treasury on limited term appointment. When that
term expired, he was without employment. Friends in
the Whig party created for him in November, 1846, the
anomalous post of "Secretary to the Postmaster General" at a salary of £1200, while Colonel Maberly remained "Secretary to the Post Office" at £2000 a year.
It was left for the two to adjust their domains as best
they might. Certainly the situation was uncomfortable;
Hill, however, was not one to make it easier, and continued energetically to try his influence to have Maberly
retired, or transferred, or induced to resign by the
offer of full salary by way of pension.[38] The conflict of
the two was somewhat amusingly carried on in the next
generation when Hill's nephew wrote the adulatory article on his uncle for the *Dictionary of National Biography*
and was likewise the authority for the disparaging one
on Maberly. When the assistant secretary died in 1848,
the Marquis of Clanricarde, the postmaster general,
"who in a matter of patronage was not scrupulous" (as
Trollope said), with a remarkable display of affability
toward Thackeray's friend Lady Blessington, raised
Thackeray's hope of obtaining the post, but bowed to
pressure from the postal establishment. "It may be said

that had Thackeray succeeded in that attempt he would surely have ruined himself," Trollope commented. On September 29, John Tilley was appointed to the assistant secretaryship.[39] Six months later, Cecilia Trollope Tilley, whose life had long been despaired of, died of consumption at their new home in Kensington. Hill was certainly at first much impressed by Trollope. Part of his reform involved the extension of rural postal deliveries, and Trollope worked very energetically in mapping out routes in the Southern District of Ireland. The nature of the work was thus described by Hill to a parliamentary committee a few years later: The surveyor determines the length of a walk a letter carrier might reasonably make in a day, arranges the walk to include as many villages and hamlets as he can, determines whether the weekly volume of letters for those places be sufficient to pay the expense (reckoning at a penny per letter), and if it be sufficient, the postmaster general establishes the route. Trollope's effectiveness is evidence of his energy: he himself walked the routes to discover what might be expected of the carriers, or, more often and more expeditiously, went over them on horseback. "It was," he said, "the ambition of my life to cover the country with rural letter-carriers."[40]

Hill praised the "prompt and satisfactory completion" of the task as "very creditable to Mr. Trollope," and borrowed him to assist another surveyor in the reorganization of rural southwest England. On August 1, 1851, he sailed from Cork to Bristol. By early December his superior in southern Ireland urgently requested his return, but he remained in Ireland only from December 21 to the following March 11; so valuable was his work on the rural routes that when those

for western England were completed he was assigned
to do the same task for South Wales. Despite further
urgent appeals from the surveyor of his Irish district,
Maberly found him most useful in Wales; moreover, "I
believe he was led to expect that his services would be
continued here for some time longer, & if therefore he
would be inconvenienced by the change, he is entitled
to every indulgence."[41] He never returned to the
Southern Ireland District. His detailed reports on the
revision of the rural posts out of Dawlish and Teignmouth in October, 1851, survive, and minutes putting
into effect his recommendations for Stratford-on-
Avon, Stroud, Banbury, Tetbury, Woodstock, Pool,
Stourbridge, Bromsgrove, Worcester, and Hereford
from February 26 to November 2, 1853, give some in-
dication of how busy he kept.[42] The postmaster general
was gratified to observe that in the districts of the revised posts "every House, however remote, is included
in some one free delivery," and Trollope himself said
that he visited nearly every house—certainly every
house of importance—in Devonshire, Cornwall, much
of Dorset, Somerset, part of Oxfordshire, Wiltshire,
Gloucestershire, Worcestershire, Herefordshire, Mon-
mouthshire, and the six southern counties of Wales.
His zeal for the service was reinforced by the wish to
augment his income with as large an allowance for
mileage as possible, and in the winter he could arrange
his routes to take in all the most interesting hunts of
the region.[43]

The rural posts figure frequently enough in the novels. The Marquis of Brotherton scornfully commented
on his brother's propensity for walking: "He ought to
have been a country letter-carrier. He would have been
as punctual as the sun, and has quite all the necessary

intellect" (*Is He Popenjoy?* chap. 41). The folks at Nun-combe Putney had less punctual service.

> The post used to come into Nuncombe Putney at about eight in the morning, carried thither by a wooden-legged man who rode a donkey. There is a general understanding that the wooden-legged men in country parishes should be employed as postmen, owing to the great steadiness of demeanour which a wooden leg is generally found to produce. . . . The one-legged man who rode his donkey into Nuncombe Putney would reach his post-office not above half an hour after his proper time; but he was very slow in stumping round the village, and seldom reached the Clock House much before ten.

Those who lived "beyond the beat of the wooden-legged postman" were obliged to "call at the post-office for their letters" (*He Knew He Was Right*, chaps. 18, 58). And then there was poor Mrs. Crump the postmistress, who had been visited by an inspector shortly before Lily Dale undertook to ask her to send the Dales' letters up to the house early.

> "Oh, letters! Drat them for letters. I wish there weren't no sich things. There was a man here yesterday with his imperence. I don't know where he come from—down from Lun'on, I b'leeve: and this was wrong, and that was wrong, and everything was wrong; and then he said he'd have me discharged the sarvice. . . . Discharged the sarvice! Tuppence farden a day. So I told 'un to dis-charge hisself, and take all the old bundles and things away upon his shoulders. Letters indeed! What business have they with post-missuses, if they cannot pay 'em better nor tuppence farden a day?" [*The Small House at Allington*, final chapter]

Hill, meanwhile, was both distrustful of Tilley and Trollope, and eager to have them on his side. In the

autumn of 1852, Trollope mentioned to Tilley an important and money-saving improvement as regards the
surveyors' districts (Hill's journals do not say what it
was), and introduced it with the words, "Now when
Brown is gone, and you are Secretary, I mean to pro-
pose the following plan." Tilley described the plan generally to Hill, and finding that he approved it, encour-
aged Trollope to write his proposal formally, in the
hope of being awarded extra payment if it were
adopted. He showed Hill both Trollope's letters (the
preliminary letter and an inquiry about the propriety of
a formal proposal)—certainly evidence of innocence,
Hill thought, and yet Tilley *might* have forgotten the
remark made in the earlier letter. Could there be "an
understanding between the two brothers that Tilley
would succeed M[aberly]," and leave Hill still an anomalous outsider? And so he asked Tilley, who assured
him that the whole remark was meaningless, though
Trollope always referred to Maberly as "Brown." Less
than a fortnight later the superintendent of the Mail
Coach Office died; Tilley hoped to procure the position
for Trollope, "who deserves promotion," said Hill, "and
who would, I doubt not, fill the office well." Hill proposed that the economies advocated by Trollope be effected by appointing a surveyor to fill the vacant superintendency and retiring two other surveyors (Trollope,
then, would benefit by promotion either to the superintendency or to one of the surveyorships). Maberly ignored the suggestion and gave the superintendency to
the former chief clerk in the Mail Coach Office, a man
of very many years' service.[44] The appointment would
have done Trollope little good: less than two years later
the Mail Coach Office went out of existence in an administrative reorganization.

Trollope was so long in England that he moved his family with him, first to Exeter, then Bristol, Carmarthen, Cheltenham, and Worcester. Exeter and Cheltenham figure significantly in his novels, the former in *He Knew He Was Right* and *Kept in the Dark,* the latter in *The American Senator* and *Mr. Scarborough's Family.* At Cheltenham (1852–53) they took lodgings in the Paragon (the home of Miss Todd in *The Bertrams* and *Miss Mackenzie*) and the boys went to school. On one occasion, about June 8, 1852, when his mission carried him to Budleigh Salterton, he called on a Winchester College contemporary, the Reverend Hay Sweet Escott, and there met the lad who was to become his first biographer. "Boy, help me on with my coat," was the only memorable remark the lad could record.[45]

A few months before Trollope went to western England the inhabitants of Jersey (which was in the Western English District) had submitted a formal memorial on their postal service to the postmaster general; in response, and as part of his special assignment, Trollope was sent to the Channel Islands from November 4–24, 1851. With his usual vigor he made his report in seventeen days—a detailed reorganization of the postmen's routes, with the establishment of two horse posts for carrying mail from St. Helier to the outlying portions of Jersey (formerly carried entirely on foot), and with provisions for more frequent delivery of letters internally, so that services were no longer keyed solely to the three weekly boats from England. Every item of cost and time was carefully calculated. The report was approved and the reorganization effected. There were difficulties in the execution; one of the sorters, for example, was a very old man who had been slow enough at best and who could not get used to the new routes.

Letters of complaint came in, and few letters of commendation. But postal arrangements never do elicit praise, Trollope replied. "People injured complain, but those who are benefitted rarely express gratification. If the horse posts were now taken away, the loss would probably be much felt."[46]

One part of Trollope's report, however, brought nothing but enthusiasm.

> There is at present no receiving office in St. Heliers, and persons living in the distant parts of the town have to send nearly a mile to the principal office. I believe that a plan has obtained in France of fitting up letter boxes in posts fixed at the road side, and it may perhaps be thought adviseable to try the operation of this system in St. Heliers—postage stamps are sold in every street, and therefore all that is wanted is a safe receptacle for letters, which shall be cleared on the morning of the despatch of the London Mails, and at such other times as may be requisite. Iron posts suited for the purpose may be erected at the corners of streets in such situations as may be desirable, or probably it may be found to be more serviceable to fix iron letter boxes about five feet from the ground, wherever permanently built walls, fit for the purpose can be found, and I think that the public may safely be invited to use such boxes for depositing their letters.

The recommendation was endorsed by John Tilley, sketches were made, an iron founder commissioned, and seven freestanding boxes were cast, four for Jersey and three for Guernsey, at a cost of £7 each. In due course posters appeared announcing to the public that the roadside letter boxes would be opened on November 23, 1852, with collections twice daily except Sunday. Within a fortnight reports came in that the inhabitants wanted more of them, especially in the rural districts. One of the boxes originally set up proved too small for the demand, and a larger design was evolved. A fifth box was set up less than a year after the first four, and this one, with the rector's consent, was let into the wall of the rector's garden.[47]

Formerly, letters could be deposited only at post offices; the use of letter boxes supposed a uniform rate of postage for letters and prepayment of postage by the sender, rather than collection from the recipient. The establishment of the penny post and the invention of the adhesive postage stamp provided the necessary conditions. Now letters could be dropped in by senders and picked up for dispatch at hours when the post offices would be closed. By the middle of the decade roadside letter boxes had spread all over the kingdom, and the number of new ones was proudly reported each year to the Commons by the postmaster general (actually, of course, by Rowland Hill, the secretary).[48] Though Trollope did not invent the pillar-box (having taken the idea from France, as he said), his simple suggestion has had an impact on the lives of everyone for more than a century. His report and his mission to the Channel Islands were especially commended by his superiors.

But he was not always ahead of his time. The hours might be stated on the box, but a patron could never be sure whether he was posting his letter on time or just too late for an advertised collection. Various indicators were proposed. Trollope's view in 1861 was that there was no need for such an indicator: *his* collectors (he was by this time a surveyor in England) kept to their time accurately, and patrons might see that their own clocks were correct. Moreover, one must not make things too complicated for the intellects of the collectors.[49] In England, though not in America, Trollope has been overruled, and each letter box indicates when the last collection has been made (or rather, when the next collection will be made).

The letter boxes became so popular that influential citizens began to clamor for their erection near their homes, and one part of the secretary's duties came to be answering such requests as were addressed to him personally by people who could claim an acquaintance with him. In May, 1865, for example, John Everett Millais, who lived at 7 Cromwell Place, London, asked Tilley to set up a pillar box in his neighborhood; the box he requested still stands on the corner of Cromwell Place and Cromwell Road, perhaps a partial reward for his having illustrated the novels of the secretary's brother-in-law.[50]

It was with a self-depreciating irony, therefore, that Trollope described the conservative stubbornness of Miss Jemima Stanbury of Exeter in *He Knew He Was Right:*

> As for the iron pillar boxes which had been erected of late years for the receipt of letters, one of which—a most hateful thing to her,—stood almost close to her own hall door, she had not the faintest belief that any letter put into one of them would ever reach its destination. She could not understand why people should not walk with their letters to a respectable post-office instead of chucking them into an iron stump—as she called it,—out in the middle of the street with nobody to look after it. Positive orders had been given that no letter from her house should ever be put into the iron post. [Chap. 8]

Soon after Trollope's return from Ireland to England in 1852, as he was wandering about Salisbury on a summer evening, there came to him the story of *The Warden,* and if Barchester is not explicitly Salisbury, the country in which he was now spending so much of his time did provide the main features of the county he created, the county of Barset. When in his *Autobiography* he claims that he had "never lived in any cathedral city,—except London, never knew anything of any Close," he was forgetting his years at Winchester College, which is adjacent to the cathedral, and where St. Cross Hospital bears some resemblance to the Hiram's Hospital that is at the center of *The Warden*. It was more than a year later—on July 29, 1853, at Tenbury in Worcestershire, as he meticulously records it—that he began the writing of the novel.[51]

The New Civil Service

Trollope had nearly completed his revision of the rural posts in South Wales when the surveyor for the Northern District of Ireland applied for leave on account of health; Trollope was directed to take charge of the district at once as acting surveyor. He arrived in Belfast on August 29, 1853, and assumed his new duties officially on September 5. There was a five-day meeting in Glasgow with the surveyors from Scotland and England beginning January 31, 1854, to revise the postal links between Ireland and the north of England; for the rest he was in Ulster until the following summer. One of the surveyor's clerks there was a kinsman of Colonel Maberly, incompetent, intemperate, and insubordinate; Trollope and Tilley were puzzled what to do when word came that the colonel had at last resigned his secretaryship for a post with the Board of Audit. Hill was now alone in charge, and young Livesay Maberly was swiftly demoted. On

October 9, 1854, Trollope became permanent surveyor for the Northern District of Ireland on the retirement of the ailing incumbent. Three months later he got permission to move his headquarters to Dublin. He left Belfast on May 2.[52]

But first there were six weeks of leave, and then he was instructed to make himself familiar once more with the postal arrangements in southern Ireland so that he might testify before a parliamentary committee looking into them. His selection to represent the Post Office at this inquiry was a mark of special confidence, and it was true, as he told the committee, that he had indeed worked throughout the whole of Ireland. His testimony (July 16–27, 1855) was exceedingly detailed, and he insisted on giving every bit of it, even when the questioner seemed eager to move on. His tone was sometimes a bit testy. But his work won him a prompt letter of approval from his superiors; Tilley first solicited from James Wilson of the Treasury a statement that Trollope had "exhibited great knowledge and efficiency as an Officer of the Department," then composed the commendation for the postmaster general to sign.[53] Before going to London, he took a house in suburban Donnybrook, at 5 Seaview Terrace. The boys went to school near Chester.[54]

His new appointment increased his basic salary from £150 to £240 a year. Almost immediately, however, a general revision of the scale brought him to the new maximum of £700, plus twenty shillings for every day away from headquarters, thirty pounds for office rent, and reimbursement of actual cost of conveyance while traveling within his district on official business. His means of official travel became increasingly the railway instead of the horse, and he soon took to spending his hours in the carriages writing; *Barchester Towers* was the first of his novels to be written largely on trains. The manuscripts of the early novels have not survived; they were written in pencil, he tells us, and then transcribed for the printer by his wife.[55] (The evangelical Sabbatarianism of Mrs. Proudie, by the way, had special overtones for Trollope, since the Post Office was under constant pressure to cease Sunday deliveries and even the handling of mails on the trains on Sundays.)

New brooms were being readied for the Civil Service in those days—brooms described at length in a blue book prepared by Sir Charles Trevelyan and Sir Stafford Northcote, with the help of Professor Benjamin Jowett; the evils of patronage would be swept away, cobwebs that had accumulated on the supine bodies of idle civil servants would be banished, and the entire service would be refurbished with the help of rigorous examinations administered by an independent board. Trollope, in Ireland, hardly knew whether to be outraged or amused. He sent a long article on the blue book to the *Dublin University Magazine*, where it was published anonymously in October, 1855. "It has for some years been apparent to us, that if a real Utopia could be peopled with emigrants from Great Britain, Sir Charles Trevelyan would be the only man to whom could be confided the chief magistracy of the colony. Sir Stafford Northcote, who rode worthily into fame on the cupola of the London Exhibition, is a fitting associate for so great an administrator."[56] (Trollope put the two men into *The Three Clerks* as Sir Gregory Hardlines and Sir Warwick Westend. Though he later came to know Sir Charles and Lady Trevelyan and to be very fond of them, and Sir Charles contributed to *St. Pauls Magazine*, the idea of the utopian colonial administrator suggests that Trevelyan's rigor was also incorporated in John Neverbend, president of Britannula in *The Fixed Period*.)

The proposed system of competitive examination, as the proponents saw it, would automatically ensure that the ablest youth of the country would be attracted to the Civil Service, but the practical Trollope commented that no one enters a competition merely for the thrill of doing well: the pay at stake was sadly deficient and there must be more ample provision for advancement. By a kind of naive self-confidence, the proponents of the scheme believed they could tell enough about the candidates through examination so that they could place them in the most suitable branch of the service, regardless of the candidate's wishes. And to prevent overspecialization, they recommended constant transfer from one branch to another, from Post Office to Admiralty to Treasury to War Office, for example. By the same logic, said Trollope, the candlestick maker should spend large portions of his life cutting meat and baking bread.

As for the subjects to be examined, they suggested that "proficiency in history, jurisprudence, political economy, modern languages, political and physical geography, and other matters, besides the staple of classics and mathematics, will be useful." "Useful!" exclaimed Trollope. These lads are seventeen years old; at what age does the English boy acquire such proficiencies?[57] And will the Civil Service ever attract such prodigies? expecially when, as now, the very highest positions—permanent secretaries, under-secretaries, chairmen, commissioners, and such like—are filled by men who have risen altogether outside the service—at the bar, very commonly—and when the proponents of the new system actually assume that such a practice is unexceptionable. The talented candidates can look forward at best to a career of anonymity, of seeing their superiors take credit for their own nameless work; those who place lower in the examination, despite their preparation in so wide a range of subjects, will have a lifetime as copyists. Civil servants cannot be brought ready-made to their work: a great deal of their training must take place after their appointment. Previous education is of course necessary, but it should be provided for in some way not at the cost of the candidate, who gambles a great deal of his life for a very slight reward.

Trollope is eloquent in denying that the civil servants of the day are as incompetent as the authors of the proposal portray them, and rejoices that a good many of the commentators upon it spoke firmly in their defense. In addition, the popular myth of "red tape" needs correction: it is based on the notion that flights of inspired genius could set all routine work to rights! "Red tape" means merely "good order."

The essay will be repeated in whole or in part, with slight modifications, whenever Trollope writes or speaks about the Civil Service. As he remarked, the worst aspect of the utopian theories advanced in the blue book was that those who advanced them might indeed be empowered to put them into practice—and so they did, with the constituting of the Civil Service Commission.

Trollope later (April 26, 1860) had to face Sir Stafford Northcote over a committee table when Northcote was questioning Tilley and Trollope about the success of the civil service examinations with respect to the Post Office. Both were firm in their opposition, and Trollope, though suffering from a sore throat, told with some indignation how a postmaster, all of whose candidates for sorter had failed the commission's examination, turned to Trollope for help; Trollope found a good man in another town, sent him over, and then beheld him too rejected by the commission—"because he could not spell. He would never [in his duties] have been called upon to spell a word!" In the end, a higher salary had to be offered only to attract a man who could pass the examination.[58]

In 1857 Trollope was invited to write a seven-page "History of the Post Office in Ireland" as part of the postmaster general's annual report. It is a lively account, anecdotal, amusing in its instances of eighteenth-century casualness about patronage, but ending with a serious boast about the efficiency of the service by the middle of the nineteenth century. "In no part of the United Kingdom has more been done for the welfare of the people by the use of railways for carrying mails and by the penny postage system than in Ireland." (Did Rowland Hill insert the phrase "by the penny postage system"?)[59]

Postal Mission to Suez

Trollope was becoming increasingly recognized as one of the most effective administrators in the department, one with a great fund of expert knowledge. When the need arose, then, to send an experienced man through the Mediterranean to Alexandria and Suez, and one of the senior English surveyors begged off the assignment, Trollope was chosen. Slightly more than a month later he was on his way: to Paris on January 30, 1858 (where he met his brother Tom), to Marseilles, then by packet (following the pattern of the mails) to Malta and on to Alexandria, which he reached on February 10.[60] Here he had two missions. One seems rather simple: might bags be used for the shipment of mails through Egypt to India, or must the letters continue to be sealed in iron boxes as they then were? Bags would be easier on the camels, but, Trollope reported, they would be subject to great friction on the camel's back and, more telling, each camel in a train of eighty or ninety had his own driver, armed with a knife and eager to rip open a mail bag. Let there be no change until the railway is completed. But the latest model of boxes (wooden rather than iron) was decidedly worse than its predecessor: they popped open easily and closed with difficulty. At least, no more of those! Once the railway from Alexandria to Suez is completed, bags should be used in the mails that go by sea from Southampton; those that travel overland through France to Marseilles may still require the security of iron boxes (though on second thought, perhaps not, for though they travel through France they are always accompanied by an Englishman). As it turned out, though no one had told Trollope, the great obstacle to bags was the quarantine regulations; once these were changed to permit bags to go through without being emptied and fumigated, iron boxes became extinct.[61]

The second mission was by far the more important: arranging a new agreement with the Egyptian government for the transfer between Alexandria and Suez of mails bound for India and Australia, an agreement needed both because of the construction of the new railway between those cities and because of the abolition of the East India Company. Trollope carefully measured the time consumed in every step of the operation (including the normal speed of a camel until the final link of the railway should be completed), and with some vigor insisted that the interest of the mails took priority over other, sometimes conflicting, interests. The steamship company wanted delays for what they pretended was the comfort of the passengers; the Egyptian Transit Administration, represented in the negotiations by Nubar Bey, wanted wider margins of time for the performance of its contracted work and was suspected of being under the thumb of the steamship company. But Trollope held to his point that the mails should be aboard ship at one port no more than twenty-four hours after the arrival of the ship at the other port. Because English mails congested the transit system by arriving at Alexandria simultaneously from Southampton and Marseilles, he agreed that the shipping schedules should be changed to space the arrivals. In the negotiations he was well supported by the acting British consul general at Alexandria. By February 23 a draft treaty had been prepared and approved by the viceroy. Trollope was then free to make a ten-day visit (March 13–23) to the Holy Land. He was homeward bound by April 4, and the actual agreement was signed by the Egyptians in June. There was a bit of crowing in a letter to Frederic Hill: "I believe that one should never give way in any thing to an Oriental. Nubar Bey, who now that the treaty is signed declares that there will be no difficulty in carrying it out, assured me at least a dozen times, that if the Viceroy insisted on his signing such an agreement he would at once abandon his office, seeing that the work to which he would be bound would be absolutely impracticable! That was the method he took to carry out the views of the Steam-packet Company's Agent." In his annual report on the Post Office for 1859, the postmaster general praised Trollope by name for his accomplishment.[62]

His work was not finished, however, with the Alexandrian negotiations: his instructions also directed him to look into the management of the post office in Malta. He spent a week there (April 9–15), then reported that even making allowance for the natural inefficiency of the Maltese, the office was overstaffed. But his sympathy for the lower orders of civil servants comes out in his recommendation that no one be dismissed; let the next vacancy not be filled, and let the money freed thereby be used to increase the salaries of the other clerks. Also, their regular hours of work were needlessly long, considering that they were often called on at irregular and inconvenient hours when the mail packets arrived. There was, moreover, in Trollope's view, an unnecessary amount of record keeping and busy work.[63]

His recommendations were approved and acted upon promptly in London. And now, having almost completed his mission, he took a six-day holiday in the south of Spain between boats at Gibraltar. There were still four days in which he could make a study of the Gibraltar post office comparable to the one he had made at Malta. He reached London on May 10.

On his way through London at the beginning of his mission he had sold to Chapman and Hall the third of his Barsetshire novels, *Doctor Thorne,* then only about half completed. The book was written on the trains, on shipboard in the most abominably rough weather, and finally in Egypt. The very day after it was finished he began *The Bertrams,* part of which was set in the Holy

Land. This first mission produced no travel book, but the two heroes of *The Bertrams* journeyed across France and the Mediterranean for no other apparent reason than to give their author the excuse to write a long chapter describing the sights of Cairo. They returned on "that gallant first-class steamer, the 'Cagliari,' " on which, it may be assumed, Trollope had sailed. Other experiences of his mission appear in the short stories he collected as *Tales of All Countries.*

The Mission to the West Indies

Rose Trollope met her husband in London and together they took a holiday at Ollerton in Sherwood Forest, not far from her former home near Sheffield and only a mile or two from Rufford Park. Then they proceeded to Scotland, where Anthony was on temporary duty revising posts for most of the period up to the middle of September. He was at his home in Donnybrook, outside Dublin, only about eight weeks before setting out on his next mission abroad, this one even more complex, and, in the judgment of his superiors, even more successful than the one to the Mediterranean.[64]

As early as 1855 the government had resolved to make all the colonial post offices except for military stations like Malta and Gibraltar independent of the General Post Office in London and to place them under local control. But the legislatures in Jamaica and British Guiana had been reluctant to authorize the transfer, partly at least because the local postal officials saw their positions threatened and therefore somewhat

disingenuously represented to the colonial legislators
that the change would greatly increase the burden of
cost locally. Trollope thus had to negotiate with the
political powers in both places. The packet services, of
course, remained under the control of London, and it
appeared that they were neither so speedy nor so inex-
pensive as they should have been, so that Trollope had
also to study every detail of the shipping arrangements.
Next, the transfer of mails across the Isthmus of Panama (or alternatively across Central America at some
other point) for the west coast of America (especially
British Columbia) and even, perhaps, for Australia and
New Zealand, had to be examined at close range in
order to secure the most advantageous arrangement.
And the Spanish islands of Cuba and Puerto Rico had
to be persuaded to reduce their charges for mail sent to
the United Kingdom. Trollope arrived in London on
November 3, 1858, for briefing. On the sixteenth he
"started in great force" (to use Tilley's words), and next
day sailed from Southampton on the steamship *Atrato,*
armed with a very long letter of instructions in which
Frederic Hill, the assistant secretary in charge of the
packet services, authorized him to travel almost at will
throughout the Caribbean area as he might find need.[65]

At St. Thomas he left the *Atrato* and traveled to
Jamaica aboard a smaller vessel, the *Derwent,* which
reached Kingston on December 6. The postal arrangements at Jamaica presented problems that in the end
could be resolved only by a broad hint that Her
Majesty's government would give up the administration of the posts there whether or not the local government was prepared to assume it. The legislature's
fear that the postal administration, if local, would be
subject to jobbery on the part of the governor was

held by Trollope to be no concern of the home government, and the local surveyor's estimate of the loss to Jamaica if the British ceased their subsidy was shown by Trollope to be largely the fiction of a man who was going to lose his position when the change was effected. Nevertheless Trollope traveled the post routes on the island and suggested certain economies that would help balance the accounts. His final letter from the island was dated January 22, 1859.[66]

Two days later he boarded the sailing brig *Linwood* for the south coast of Cuba, having been assured that there would be great saving of time if he traveled by sea only to Cienfuegos and then overland to Havana. But he and his advisers had reckoned without the wind: "We have been becalmed half the time since, and I shall lose more time than I shall gain," he wrote to his mother from the vessel on the twenty-seventh. "I believe that in these days a man should never be tempted to leave the steamboats." Nevertheless, he had another reason for undertaking the voyage over this route: to see whether, when the railway under construction between Cienfuegos and Havana was completed, it might be more economical to send the mails there from Jamaica instead of sailing round to the north coast of Cuba. His book on the West Indies, which he proposed to his publishers from Jamaica on January 11, begins aboard the brig with a most eloquent echo of the Ancient Mariner's outcry against the calm and the heat.[67]

From Cuba he went back to St. Thomas, then on the route along the Windward Islands to Barbados, St. Vincent, Grenada, Trinidad, and British Guiana, then again to St. Thomas aboard "that most horrid of all steamvessels, the *Prince*," to take another vessel for Santa Martha (in New Granada, or Colombia), Cartagena, and Aspinwall or Colon. A part of his instructions had been to prod the postmaster at Demerara, a veteran in the service who had grown very slack about remitting the public money that came into his hand, and to report upon the postmistress at Grenada, "who has occasioned a great deal of trouble to the London office by the manner in which she has performed her duties, and who has shewn very slight signs of improvement."[68]

The negotiations in Panama were twofold: an attempt to persuade the authorities of New Granada to abrogate the tax they were levying on all British transit mails and an attempt to arrive at a less costly contract with the Panama Railroad Company for the conveyance. The shortest way to handle the former problem was to follow the example of the United States and simply refuse to pay the tax, since the government of New Granada was too remote and too weak to enforce the payment. But there was some need to retain their good will, and Trollope learned from the local government officials that a substantial reduction could be at once negotiated. By the end of December a new treaty was signed in London. As for the railway company, the expenses of their operation were such that Trollope found their charges not excessive; nevertheless he did obtain from them a reiteration of a previous offer to transport all mails, regardless of weight, for a flat annual fee, should the volume warrant entering into such an arrangement.[69]

The British man-of-war *Vixen* then took him up the Pacific to Costa Rica, to inspect the route of a proposed canal across Central America; he himself crossed, under the most primitive conditions, to Greytown (San Juan del Norte), where he was picked up by the *Trent* and returned to Colon. He remained skeptical about the feasibility of a canal, though undoubtedly the route through the Nicaraguan lakes and the San Juan River of Costa Rica was the best. But "all mankind has heard much of M. Lesseps and his [proposed] Suez canal. . . . I have a very strong opinion that such a canal will not and cannot be made," and the eloquence of other French projectors in Central America left him unconvinced. Trollope was sensitive to the prospect for change in the entire region; he knew, for example, of Yankee territorial greed and the decay of the Spanish empire, and even expressed the opinion that it would perhaps be best if Cuba should become an American possession. But he had no way of knowing that the United States was on the brink of a civil war, that the *Trent* was to figure in the international crisis that had all America and Britain by the ears the next time he visited the States, or that the American frigate *Merrimac,* aboard which he was a guest at Panama, was to become the mainstay of the Confederate fleet and, sheathed in iron, was to fight a famous battle in Hampton Roads with the little cheesebox *Monitor.*[70]

At San José Trollope attempted to see the British Envoy Extraordinary, Sir William Ouseley, and sent his card by a servant to Sir William's secretary, whose response, loud enough to be heard, was, "Oh, tell Mr. Trollope to go to the devil. It's much too hot to see anyone!" In fact, Trollope was soon taking over the secretary's living quarters, and the man, William Webb Follet Synge, became a lifelong friend. He had already met Thackeray in the United States, and it was not many years later that Trollope and Thackeray rescued Synge in a desperate moment with the loan of nearly two thousand pounds, a sum Thackeray did not live to see fully repaid.[71]

From Panama Trollope went once again to St. Thomas, whence he journeyed to Bermuda aboard the *Delta*, and thence by sailing vessel, the *Henrietta*, to New York; it was the only means of transportation between the two places. He had time only for a quick visit to Niagara Falls before catching the Cunarder *Africa* for Liverpool, which he reached on July 4.[72]

The boldest and most significant of Trollope's recommendations was not made until his return to London. "In these latitudes the respectable, comfortable, well-to-do route from every place to every other place is via the little Danish island of St. Thomas . . . —or [was so] when this was written," he said in *The West Indies*, with an eye to the change he hoped to effect. "The Royal Mail Steam Packet Company dispense all their branches from that favoured spot." Trollope's report of July 16 was to recommend making Jamaica the center of distribution instead of St. Thomas. Thus the mails would travel a greater part of their way to their ultimate destination on the faster transatlantic vessels, there would no longer be a multiplying of distances by conveying mails from St. Thomas to Jamaica, Havana, and Panama on vessels traveling nearly parallel courses as far as Jamaica, the transfer point would be on British soil, to the greater prosperity of the Jamaicans, and the large contingent of Englishmen engaged in handling the mails would be removed from, "as I believe it to be, the most pestilential harbour in the West Indies." "As far as I have been able to learn, the harbour of St. Thomas—not the island on shore—is more subject to yellow fever than any other thickly inhabited spot in the West Indies. The officers employed in the intercolonial service of the company are all sent out as very young men, and the service is one to them of much danger." St. Thomas would be reduced to a coaling station, and while coal was being taken on, the mails for the nearby Windward Islands and Demerara (British Guiana) could be transferred to a smaller vessel. The whole of Trollope's report on this matter shows that he had spent his voyage outward not merely finishing *The Bertrams* but also talking to the officers of his ship about such technical matters as the effect of prevailing winds on the speed of vessels of different sizes, the condition of navigable passages between islands, and the location of suitable alternate harbors. His meticulous calculation indicated a saving of 3,500 miles a month over the packet company's plan, or (at the rate at which mileage was calculated) more than £15,000 a year. When the packet company's representatives in London demurred at his proposals, Trollope went into even greater detail, and urged an appeal to the Admiralty, whose hydrographer replied: "I entirely concur in Mr. Trollope's proposal and recommend that it be carried into effect as early as sufficient notice of the changes can be given." The Treasury also concurred in a preference for Jamaica as the central station in the West Indies.

The packet company prevailed, presumably because they feared their commercial interests would suffer from the change, but the weight of Trollope's demonstration hung over them in the performance of their mail services, with the threat that if their own scheme for acceleration did not prove satisfactory, they would find the change forced upon them. The postmaster general's next annual report fairly glowed with pride in Trollope's achievement, "although a landsman"![73]

The Eastern District of England

From Liverpool Trollope hastened to his family in Donnybrook for a brief visit, then on the twelfth of July, 1859, he went to London to write his reports, and while there secured for himself the surveyorship of the Eastern District of England, in the place of a man who was retiring. The appointment was not official until January 10, 1860; nevertheless, by August 2 he announced proudly to his wife that she was to be mistress of Waltham House at Waltham Cross, in Hertfordshire on the boundaries of Essex and Middlesex, in his new district—a house he took on lease but subsequently bought. After a six-week holiday in the Pyrenees with Rose, he returned to Ireland to wind up his affairs there and by mid-November had moved to his new home. During this busy late summer and autumn he was also asked to observe at first hand a system of "restricted sorting" in Glasgow, Liverpool, and Manchester in order to introduce it in Dublin, and early in December he helped in reorganizing the postal establishments for Liverpool, Manchester, and Birmingham.

His district was essentially Essex, Suffolk, Norfolk, Cambridge, and Huntingdonshire, with the eastern edge of Bedfordshire and Hertfordshire on a line that included Biggleswade, Hitchin, Hatfield, and Barnet. The first novel he began after his transfer, *Orley Farm,* was set in his new district, and so too were many subsequent ones, including a large portion of *The Way We Live Now.* Place-names like Clavering and Ongar, in *The Claverings,* though not there used in their actual geographical sense, are drawn from the district, and so is Belton of *The Belton Estate*.[74]

Trollope's routine duties are reflected in the memoranda preserved in the minute books. A junior clerk in the Colchester post office was suspended for a week for carelessness, on Trollope's report, and warned to mend his ways. The postmaster at Yarmouth was reimbursed for fitting up a temporary office. A new pillar-box was erected at Thetford and the messenger's wages were raised two shillings a week for making collections from it. On the other hand, two letter boxes requested by postal patrons in Saffron Walden were disapproved by him and not erected. Rural postmen from Bury St. Edmunds whose walks were sixteen miles daily had their wages increased from twelve to fourteen shillings a week. An ancillary letter carrier at Bury was promoted to letter carrier and stamper. Trollope proposed a new arrangement for the post town serving Narborough and Pentney. The postmaster of Newmarket was required to resign, but the new appointee, despite Trollope's recommendation, was not granted an increased stipend. Rural deliveries in the neighborhood of Enfield were rearranged on his recommendation, as were those for Ongar and the areas round Romford and Brentwood. Several postmasters' salaries were increased, though in one instance a clerk's position was left vacant and the postmaster was required to assume his duties.[75]

His replies to complaints and suggestions have augmented the stocks of autograph collectors. He explained to the M.P. for Hertfordshire who had forwarded a memorial from some constituents that a later hour for the mail cart through Much Hadham to Bishop's Stortford would delay the posts at the latter place and could not be granted. Lady Stradbroke had to be told that the postmaster at Wangford, for whom she interceded, had held the office so long that he had regarded it as a right and absolutely neglected his duties despite warnings, so that a new one had been appointed. Sir Bartle Frere's brother seemed to have no ground for complaint about a letter's taking two days from Diss to Kenninghall: it had been posted too late. The rector of Skeyton was told that it would be too expensive to send a messenger to collect from a pillar-box he wanted erected in his parish. Trollope would call upon the vicar of Runham to ascertain the circumstances of his complaint. Captain Henry Byng, R.N. (of the family of the admiral executed *pour encourager les autres*) had written on behalf of Cook the mail cart contractor; but Cook had been going slower and slower, and so his contract had been canceled. If he should submit a new tender competitive with others, it would be accepted and the experience would be sure to speed him up.[76] One of Trollope's earliest moves in his new district brought him one of his earliest complaints. Seeing that there were more letters per day for East Bergholt than for Lawford, Trollope had reversed the circuit for delivery out of Manningtree so that it went to East Bergholt first and Lawford last. This was by no means satisfactory to the rector of Lawford, Charles Merivale, older brother of the John Merivale with whom Trollope had explored the abandoned mansion that inspired *The Macdermots*. The two had not met since Charles Merivale left Harrow in 1824, though Trollope had on two occasions reviewed parts of Merivale's *History of the Romans under the Empire* for the *Dublin University Magazine* (May 1851 and July 1856). The present grievance served to renew the acquaintance. A few years later (1866), at Trollope's suggestion, Merivale joined him as a member of the committee of the Royal Literary Fund. But on postal matters Merivale continued to grumble: "The P. O. is constantly blundering, notwithstanding . . . the numerous complaints I make myself to Trollope about it," he wrote to his mother.[77]

The Committee of Inquiry

Sir Rowland Hill was absent on prolonged sick leave when the *Times* on March 29–30, 1860, published a long article on the shortcomings of the Post Office, especially in the metropolitan area, and urged a parliamentary inquiry. "Want of room, want of improved system, and want of a properly paid and efficient staff, are fast giving rise to such disorganization as almost calls for the interference of the Legislature." The accusations were that the Post Office regarded itself as a source of revenue, not as a service, and that the lower staff—the people who actually handled the letters—were underpaid and overworked. Tilley, as assistant secretary, instantly requested comments from the responsible officers, and at the suggestion of William Bokenham, controller of the Circulation Department, recommended to Lord Elgin, the postmaster general, appointment of a committee from the Post Office to examine the charges; Bokenham and Thomas Boucher of the Circulation Department, Frank Ives Scudamore, the receiver and accountant general, R. Parkhurst of the Secretary's Department, and Trollope were named on April 2. Group after group of the Post

Office workers filed petitions to be heard by the committee, and the unrest grew to a point where Tilley needed reassurance from Boucher that it would not reach the proportions of a strike.[78]

But Sir Rowland Hill in his seclusion saw matters slipping out of his control. First of all (obviously after consultation with him) his brother Frederic, an assistant secretary nominally on a par with Tilley but several years his junior in appointment, instructed the committee "not to take any steps which they have any reason to believe would not be approved by both the Assistant Secretaries, without first reporting the case for instructions." Instantly the committee resigned. Tilley furiously asserted his seniority to F. Hill and urged that the resignations be not accepted. Three days later (April 24) Sir Rowland suspended the committee. Fears of the workers' discontent then became urgent, and on April 30 Sir Rowland instructed the committee to get back to work, under certain restrictions. The committee insisted that it would not do so without assurance that its inquiry might be unfettered, and Frederic Hill responded that unless they took up their task they would be regarded as disobeying their chief's instructions. Trollope's signature of course appears on each statement issued by the committee in this interchange.

The committee of inquiry was then reconstituted to include two representatives of the Treasury, which after all would have to approve any measures that involved salaries; Boucher stepped down but Trollope remained. Bokenham in a printed flyer assured the employees that the committee would begin its investigation without delay and warned that they must abstain from "any proceedings tending to agitation, or inconsistent with the rules of the Department, in respect of the form in which their representations should be brought before" their superiors. Deliberations of the committee began on May 16, and in seventeen sessions over the next seven weeks the committee examined 116 witnesses, 92 of them delegates of the postal employees' groups who had signed memorials to the committee. One of the many complaints was the system of spying on suspected pilferers and entrapment through marked currency; Trollope moved from the committee table to the witness's chair to describe the system of "restrictive sorting" whereby all the contents of a single letter box went through the hands of only four people in the post office, so that responsibility could be fixed without espionage. On July 21 the committee completed its twenty-seven page report, with recommendations for significant improvements in salary scale for the lower employees, and accompanied it with a printed transcript of evidence and memorials that ran to 342 folio pages. Sir Rowland urged the postmaster general of the new government, Lord Stanley of Alderley, to let all but the least complex of the committee's proposals wait for adoption until his return from his leave of absence.

Sir Rowland in fact regarded the committee and its operations as a "cabal" against him. From his Hampstead home on January 16, 1861, he sent a long and severe stricture on the work of the committee, with some bitter personal remarks on Tilley, whom he blamed for the entire inquiry and accused of thereby letting the discipline of the service collapse.[79] The committee was reconvened to reply to Hill on February 28; Tilley defended himself, and Lord Stanley of Alderley affirmed that it was not Tilley but the postmaster general who had the responsibility for naming and commissioning the body (a bit of fiction, of course; the postmaster general acted on Tilley's advice).

Meanwhile, on January 4 Trollope had given the first of a series of fortnightly lectures at the Post Office by various literary men to raise money for the Post Office library; his topic was hardly literary—"The Civil Service as a Profession"—and the lecture was fully reported in the newspapers next day. It was an open challenge to Hill on one issue:

> If any plan could enable a job-loving senior to withstand the spirit of the age and put unfairly forward his special friends, it was the system of promotion by merit as at present sanctioned. . . . I trust we shall live to see it overthrown, or rather to overthrow it—(cheers). . . . The question should not have been decided for us without an expression of the opinion of the profession in general. (Cheers.) Such an expression might easily have been elicited; but that had not been done, and an enormous change had been made affecting all our worldly interests with an importance that could not be exaggerated. And that change had been made without any attention to the wishes of the profession and so made in accordance with the Utopian theories of a very few men.

Now one of Sir Rowland's proudest accomplishments was (in the words of his nephew's article on him in the *Dictionary of National Biography*) that "by establishing promotion by merit he had breathed fresh life into every branch of the service." And so Hill informed Trollope that the postmaster general had expressed disapproval of the lecture (the disapproval of course put into his mouth by Hill.)[80]

Then Trollope published the lecture in the February number of the *Cornhill.* Hill first told Tilley that, though its publication in a time of latent insubordination in the secretary's office might be incendiary, he did not blame Tilley for not rebuking Trollope, "considering his position with reference to Trollope." He then asked Lord Stanley of Alderley to censure Trollope officially, but Stanley confessed that Trollope had shown him the article in proofs a fortnight earlier, and so he was in no position to speak. More than a year later, Hill wrote in his diary:

> Matthew [Hill] has had a correspondence with Trollope. T. takes the opportunity of speaking highly of me, and of defending his own conduct. Don't believe in T's sincerity—no man both clever and honest could be a party to the elaborate misrepresentations in the two Reports of the Committee on the Circulation office, and as T. is undoubtedly clever, it follows in my opinion that he is dishonest.—E[dward] Page to whom I mentioned the circumstance assures me, also in confidence, that T. has recently spoken of me in his presence, in a manner quite inconsistent with his present professions.[81]

The issue of promotion by merit was resolved, even before Sir Rowland retired, in accordance with Trollope's views. Tilley agreed with him at least insofar as assenting to the proposition that the superior officers could have little opportunity of assessing in detail the respective merits of a large number of the employees in the lower ranks. Tilley and Trollope on April 26, 1860, had testified together before a parliamentary select committee on civil service appointments (an appearance that had been deferred three days because of the urgency surrounding the constitution of the Post Office's committee of inquiry). Their testimony was largely concerned with Trollope's old bugaboo of the inappropriateness of the Civil Service Commission's examinations to the posts that the examinees were to fill. But the other matter was very much in the background. The promotion on April 10 of two clerks to higher ranks over the heads of three (in one case) and six (in the other) men senior to them led to a memorial to the postmaster general in protest, signed by a large number of clerks in three departments; the memorial was one of those placed before the committee of inquiry. The postmaster general requested that heads of departments be canvassed for their opinions, and Trollope on June 13 replied briefly: "Excepting always Staff appointments, . . . I think that all promotion should go by seniority, *and as a matter of right*, a certificate of general competence being only required." Tilley's advice to the postmaster general led to the formulation of a policy that directly contravened Hill's convictions: at the lower levels, promotion would be by seniority, provided the competence of a man for the new level was assured; for the highest positions, promotion by merit was to be maintained. " 'Promotion by merit' looks well on paper," Tilley wrote, ". . . but I believe that, if it be adhered to, you will in a few years, have an amount of dissatisfaction and indifference in your Public Offices that will be very difficult to contend with. Even in the higher grades of the service it is sometimes nearly impossible to decide who is positively the best man."[82]

The question arose once more three years later; heads of departments were again canvassed to see if they retained their former opinions, and Trollope once again (May 24, 1863) affirmed his conviction, this time at greater length: "I feel very sure that the system of promotion by merit, as it is called, cannot in truth be carried out; and that it is injurious to the service. . . . The system demands that promotion shall be given to

the best man, let the merits of those who are to be
superseded be what they may,—and let the years of
service and well-grounded expectations of the senior
candidates be also what they may." No matter how long
a man has worked, giving his best services; no matter
that he may have married on the assured conviction of
his promotion; no matter that he is perfectly fit for a
higher place, he may lose it all if someone better come
along at the last minute. "No amount of excellence is
safe, because a greater amount of excellence must always be possible." "To know whether a man be absolutely fit or unfit for certain duties is within the capacity of an observant and intelligent officer;—but it is
frequently altogether beyond the capacity of any officer however intelligent and observant to say who is
most fit. Zeal recommends itself to one man, intelli-
gence to a second, alacrity to a third, punctuality to a
fourth, and superficial pretense to a fifth. There can be
no standard by which the excellence of men can be
judged as is the weight of gold." And what of the good
men who are cruelly passed over under this system?
"The man who is competent and has exerted himself
and is yet passed over, cannot but be broken-hearted;
and from a broken-hearted man no good work can be
obtained."

On March 1, 1864, the news reached Trollope that
Hill had resigned; at the same time a copy of Hill's
revised pamphlet on *Results of Postal Reform* came to
him from the author. He wrote courteously the next
day:

> I cannot but have felt for the last year or two since I
> was called upon to make one of a committee of inquiry
> during your illness, that you have regarded me as being
> in some sort unfriendly to your plans of postal reform.

I am not going to trouble you with any discussion on
that matter, but I cannot let your resignation from office pass without assuring you of my thorough admira-
tion for the great work of your life. . . . There are national services, for which a man can receive no adequate
reward, either in rank or money, and it has been your
lot to render such a service to the world at large. I hope
that you may live long to enjoy the recognition of your
own success.

The courtesy not unnaturally gave pleasure: "Among
the numerous letters of congratulation are . . . some
even from men whom I have had too much reason to
believe unfriendly," Hill wrote in his journal. "There is
an excellent letter, among others, from Trollope." But
Trollope's personal judgment of Hill as an administrative officer remained what it had always been, and
when after both men were dead his expression of that
opinion was made public in *An Autobiography,* Hill's son,
zealous like all members of the family for Sir Rowland's
glory, published this letter. No reader of Hill's private
journals can think other than that, for all Hill's great
service to the world, rewarded ultimately with burial in
Westminster Abbey, Trollope's judgment of him was
right. He was vain and suspicious almost to paranoia,
and such a man might indeed "have put the great department with which he was concerned altogether out
of gear . . . , had he not been at last controlled."[83]

Frederic Hill continued in his position for some years
after Sir Rowland's resignation; he sometimes attempted by devious means to thwart the new secretary's
administration and he conveyed to his brother the news
of events at the Post Office. Trollope is said to have told
a story about him that was passed on in the memoirs of
another Post Office man. By way of cementing a peace
after recent quarrels, Frederic Hill invited Trollope to

dinner at his Hampstead home. When Trollope arrived, he found that he and his host were the only men in a company of twenty or thirty ladies—who, moreover, had already dined. Host and guest went down to dinner, where the only viands were part of a cold leg of mutton at one end of the table and a salad at the other—no potatoes, no other vegetables, not a drop even of water to drink. Hill told Trollope to sit opposite the mutton, and he himself sat by the salad, which he devoured entire while Trollope made the most of the mutton. They then went upstairs to the drawing room, where the ladies were seated in a huge circle with a chair in the middle for the principal guest. "The ladies will now proceed to interrogate you upon various matters," said Frederic Hill—and they did. What the matters were, the story does not tell.[84]

Leave of Absence

At the beginning of 1860 the publisher George Smith launched one of the most successful periodicals of the century, the *Cornhill Magazine,* with Thackeray as editor and a newly commissioned novel by Trollope, *Framley Parsonage,* as its principal attraction. Smith was so pleased to have Trollope among his authors that (with an eye on the success of the book on the West Indies) he made a proposal only a few months later that fairly staggered Trollope: he would pay £3000 for a book on India, two volumes of 450 pages each, plus three articles on India for the *Cornhill;* £1800 for a novel to be published in monthly parts from July 1, 1861, to June 1, 1862, and then in three volumes, and £600 for a short serial novel for the *Cornhill* in 1862. Trollope would be obliged to take leave from the Post Office to pay a visit to India, but even allowing for the loss of Post Office salary for nine months and his expenses (£1500), this contract would add close to £2000 a year for 1861 and 1862 and thereby nearly double his income.[85]

It was a tempting offer, but there were obstacles. He had just agreed with Chapman and Hall for *Orley Farm* to be issued in twenty parts in 1861–62 for £2500 and was not disposed to break the agreement. "I should certainly like to do the India book—but will not break my heart if the plan falls to the ground. Per se going to India is a bore—but it wd certainly suit me professionally."[86] In the end, the only part of the proposal that did not fall to the ground was the short serial, *The Struggles of Brown, Jones, and Robinson,* a work he had begun in August, 1857, and abandoned after only a few pages; he resumed it, and it appeared in the *Cornhill* from August, 1861, to March, 1862. Trollope's contrast, in his lecture on "The Civil Service as a Profession," between the manliness and honesty possible for a civil servant and the dishonesty often imposed on tradesmen and advertisers makes clear that *Brown, Jones, and Robinson* was meant to show the other side of the coin from *The Three Clerks.* Tom Trollope expressed his regret that the Indian scheme was abandoned: "I feel confident that the book would have improved your literary position, and given you a standing among government men, and such like, which the most successful novel-writing will not do."[87]

If India would have been a bore, America with its civil war was quite another matter. On March 20, 1861, he signed an agreement with Chapman and Hall for a book on North America, of the same size as that earlier proposed on India, and for a comparable sum of money (the copyright provisions were somewhat different, so that the outright initial payment to Trollope was only £2000).[88] Then came the need to request a leave of absence from his post.

"There is, so far as I am aware, no precedent for such an application as the enclosed from Mr. Trollope, and I need not add that an absence of seven months on the part of a Surveyor is in many respects objectionable," wrote Sir Rowland Hill on April 9 in laying the request before the postmaster general, thereby setting in motion one of the more humiliating episodes in his conflict with Trollope. Hill proposed that, in consideration of Trollope's valuable service in Egypt and the West Indies, the leave might be granted "with the distinct understanding that the indulgence be considered a full compensation for the special services on which he rests his claim." Lord Stanley of Alderley, instead of merely initialing Hill's memorandum, raised the question whether Trollope might help bring to a conclusion some of the current negotiations over postal arrangements between England and the United States, and indeed whether he might not gain valuable information for coming to an understanding with both North and South should the two finally be separated. "The employment of Mr. Trollope in the duties described above would be objectionable," replied Hill on April 12, and Stanley then initialed the original memorandum.[89]

It would appear that he had intended to approve the leave, but not the conditions Hill had stated; Hill took the initials as approving the entire memorandum and imposed those conditions. Trollope protested. On April 23 Stanley wrote to Hill:

I consider that the valuable services rendered by Mr. Trollope to the Department, justified me in granting the leave requested, though somewhat out of the ordinary course. I never thought that Mr. Trollope made any claim for compensation, nor did I intend that the Leave now granted should be considered as such. Mr. Trollope's services discharged with Zeal Diligence & Ability will always give him that claim to consideration, which the exhibition of such Qualities must entitle any officer to expect from the PMG, and the leave now granted can in no respect be considered as diminishing such claims on the part of Mr. Trollope.

One must have some awareness of the normal relation between secretary and postmaster general to sense the force of the rebuff to Hill: the postmaster general conventionally did not reverse his secretary, and perhaps nowhere else in the minute books has so firm a tone been taken, and at such length, against a secretary. Probably, though the evidence does not exist, Tilley had intervened with Stanley behind Hill's back; Trollope himself said, in *An Autobiography*, that before making the application at all in official form, he had laid his plan before the postmaster general. In any case Hill remembered the wound. "*Trollope* is suspected of neglecting his official duties to attend to his literary labours," he wrote in his journal on September 6, 1862 (after some earlier complaints about remarks Trollope was reported to have made in America disparaging the penny post). "Engagement in connection with the Cornhill Magazine and another periodical whose name I do not recollect—numerous novels—Trip to the United States . . . and work thereon—In confirmation see in Athenaeum of this day letter from Trollope in which he speaks of earning 'his bread by writing'—as though literature were his 'profession' &c."[90] It should be added that conflict with Lord Stanley of Alderley was one of the principal causes of Hill's retirement in 1864.

North America is a massive book, primarily an account of a country adjusting to secession and civil war. (Trollope did not get into the Confederate states.) But in all the more important cities he looked in at the post office and an extensive chapter examines the postal system of the United States.

Clearly, in Trollope's view, the Americans had much to learn about the management of a postal service. Nowhere was there free delivery of mail; in the larger towns deliveries might be effected by private contractors who charged the recipients for the delivery, but in Chicago even this arrangement was on the verge of collapse. The normal practice was for people to inquire for their mail at a general delivery window of the post office, or to hire a post office box; provision of space for the boxes and for the window clerks made the post office buildings large and cumbersome—that at Chicago devoted four times as much space to these matters as the post office in Liverpool, a city three times the size. In the city of Washington there was no place to purchase stamps except at a window in the post office, and there were no pillar-boxes for the deposit of letters, though these existed in other cities. Since the ordinary citizen would not trudge to the post office to inquire for letters unless he had reason to suppose some were there, the ordinary citizen was in fact not served by the post office, and the volume of letter mail in the United States was far less than half that of Britain, though the population was only two million short of the twenty-nine million inhabitants of the British Isles.

Moreover, whereas in Britain the arrival and depar-

ture of mail trains were entirely under the control of
the Post Office, in the United States the schedules were
controlled by the railroads, which had no interest what-
soever in convenient connections for the transmission
of mail. Finally, the excessive use of franking privileges
by members of Congress placed a profitless burden on
the system, and the potential dismissal of every post
office employee every four years with a change of administration was of course an insuperable obstacle to
the building up of a responsible and dedicated civil
service.

Nevertheless, the vast area of the States made for
problems the tidier British postal service never had to
face. Distances were incomparably greater, populations
less dense. There were nearly thirty thousand post offices in the states that remained in the union, in com-
parison with eleven thousand four hundred in Great
Britain. (Americans may be struck by the information
that the southern states continued to be served by the
United States Post Office until the end of May, 1861.)
Though the letter postage in America was 50 percent
higher than in Britain (except for distances above 3,000
miles, where it was five times greater), the United States
Post Office had an annual deficit of well over two million dollars, whereas the British Post Office showed a
net annual profit of over half a million dollars.

Even in smaller matters the efficient Trollope could
fancy himself putting the American system to rights—
by cutting back drastically the use of needless forms
and the making of millions of entries no one would
ever look at; by making the mail bags less expensive
and by using smaller ones where smaller ones would
serve. His American journey was a vast exercise in the
application of his professional wisdom to the needs of a

new world—one which, however, could not be expected to heed him.[91]

The Assistant Secretaryship

"I have appointed Mr. Tilley, who was the senior assistant secretary, to succeed Sir Rowland Hill, and the place vacated by him has been filled up by the promotion of Mr. Scudamore, who, amongst other able men whose claims I fully considered, seemed to me to possess the highest qualifications for the office." This was the language of the annual report of the postmaster general (still Lord Stanley of Alderley) in 1864, announcing Hill's retirement as secretary because of failing health. Tilley's appointment was hardly a surprise; for several years as assistant secretary he had carried the greater part of Hill's burden and he was the senior man in the office. For the first time in Trollope's experience, moreover, a secretary had been appointed who had risen through the ranks. But the appointment of Frank Ives Scudamore was a surprise: he was from quite another branch of the Post Office, the receiver and accountant general's office, though he had been seconded to the secretary's office on special assignment. Trollope was sadly disappointed at not securing the assistant secretaryship for himself, and his firmest principles respecting the service were offended by the appointment over him of someone six years his junior.[92] That Scudamore was an excellent administrator was beside the point.

Much to the point, however, was Trollope's sense that Tilley had been responsible for the selection. The postmaster general—who came and went with the changes of party in power—could exercise authority if he wished, but almost invariably accepted the advice of his permanent secretary, the highest continuing officer in the Post Office. Indeed, it was Tilley who wrote the annual report, the language of which has just been quoted. Tilley was one of Trollope's oldest friends; his first wife had been Trollope's sister and his second wife was also connected with the Trollopes. The strain in the relationship was not long in showing itself.

Nearly a decade earlier, on April 17, 1855, the English surveyors had sent a memorial to the postmaster general protesting that their salaries had been set at a scale £100 per annum lower than those of the heads of departments in London, though their work was fully as responsible. Tilley, acting for Hill, recommended that their protest be rejected. Again in May, 1859, the English surveyors requested equality in salary with the heads of departments, and again Tilley advised against honoring their request. Trollope was not party to these petitions, since he was still in Ireland.[93] But he was present at a meeting of the nine English surveyors at Bedford on April 6–8, 1864, and signed the memorial they there framed. By this time they could protest not only the difference in the established scale, but also the fact that it had recently "been found expedient to encrease by special allowances the Salaries of all these officers" (i.e., heads of departments and assistant secretaries) in so general a manner that it appeared a matter of policy, but the surveyors had enjoyed none of these increases. With the authorization of Lord Stanley, Tilley responded to the surveyors as a group that there had been no such general policy—that every increase beyond the scale had been for special services, and that a general revision of salaries was not to be undertaken. He seems to have felt no embarrassment in the fact that he himself had benefited from such special increments.[94]

Trollope expected the surveyors to be convened as a body to consider this reply, and when no meeting was called he addressed, on July 8, a very long letter to the secretary protesting both the decision itself and the apparently calculated rudeness with which the argument of the surveyors was brushed aside. There are many signs of haste in the letter; though nominally addressed to the secretary as "you," it refers to "Mr. Tilley" in the third person. "I do not think he will for a moment assert,—otherwise than with the general latitude of loose official phraseology, that he, as assistant Secretary, performed any special services. He did his work that was not special in a way that by the consent of all of us deserved the reward it has received; and, no doubt, before that supplemental allowance was awarded to him, he was paid insufficiently for the ordinary work of his office." "Special services were alleged,—but I am not aware, nor as far as I know is any Gentleman in the department aware, that special services had been rendered,—except by Mr. Scudamore, the late Receiver and Accountant General, whose great services on the part of the Crown have been altogether exceptional." When special circumstances are alleged as a reason for widespread, but still selective, increases, the extra payments "are in every way objectionable. They lead to endless heartburns and jealousies. They are given,—and must be ever given when given,—in a spirit of partisanship. And they are unjust alike to the department and to the public." Trollope was right, and Tilley, who was under no illusions about how the criterion of "merit" was used in the public service, must have known he was

right, had he not been understandably offended by
other parts of the letter. "I have served under the Secretaryship [as had Tilley, of course] of Sir F. Freeling,
Colonel Maberly, and Sir Rowland Hill," Trollope went
on, "and I feel assured that no application from the
whole corps of Surveyors would have been answered in
so studiously offensive a manner [Tilley underscored
these last four words when he read the letter] by either
of those Gentlemen. . . . I also think that I am justified
in asking his Lordship to recommend the newly appointed Secretary to be more considerate of the feelings
of those Officers among whom he passed his official life,
till he received his promotion."[95]

"I send to your Lordship for perusal before submit-
ting it to you officially this most intemperate letter
from Mr. Trollope," wrote Tilley to Stanley, and then,
to Trollope:

> His Lordship is at a loss to understand why you should
> come forward alone to question a circular letter which
> was addressed to yourself as only one of a body. He can
> only conclude that none of your colleagues felt ag-
> grieved or if they did that no one else could be found to
> put his signature to a document such as [Tilley first
> wrote "so improperly worded as"] that which you have
> forwarded. Be that as it may, Lord Stanley . . . desires
> me to express his regret at its tone and at the temper
> which you have displayed and to say that you have ad-
> duced no reasons which appear to him to call for a
> reconsideration of his decision.

Such was the weak reply that Tilley drafted; Lord
Stanley gave it his approval.[96]

Now Trollope attempted to take his case to the postmaster general directly, with a letter of July 18 from a
holiday in Windermere. He was, after all, on terms of
personal friendship with Lord Stanley, at whose house

he was an occasional dinner guest; they had laughed together over Sir Rowland Hill's indignation at the Post Office lecture on the Civil Service.[97] Tilley's reply to the surveyors' petition, he wrote, had studiously ignored the merits of their argument. "It was exactly the way in which Oliver was treated when he came forward on behalf of the Charity boys to ask for more;—and I own that I thought Mr. Tilley was very like Bumble in the style of the answer he gave us." There was of course no such thing as addressing the postmaster general directly; the letter went to Tilley, as Trollope knew it would, and Tilley replied that the postmaster general had nothing to add to his earlier communication. And there the matter was dropped.

It is painful to see two old and dear friends in a conflict of this sort. If Trollope may seem to have been unnecessarily aggressive and personal, it must also be observed that he was right in his argument. He wrote to an associate that, while reluctant to take such a course without listening to the advice of his friends, "My feeling is that a man should fight to the last if he feels himself to be right."[98] And there can have been nothing more frustrating than to know that there was no appeal: that Tilley was at every point putting his own words into the mouth of the postmaster general, and that unless Tilley were disposed to admit that he had been in error, there was no chance that Trollope's cause could gain a hearing. It might be added that Tilley's stance got its just response—letters from individual surveyors making claims on their own behalfs for supplementary increases in salary for "special services." Trollope made no such application.[99]

A few months later (February 10, 1865), Tilley proposed that Trollope be sent on an official mission of nine months to Gibraltar and Malta, Egypt, Bombay and possibly Calcutta, Ceylon, Shanghai, and Japan. It was clearly something he thought Trollope would enjoy and Trollope's first disposition was to accept; after nearly a fortnight's consideration, however, he declined. But all was well again between him and Tilley, and Tilley's letters resumed their affectionate form of address—"My dear Tony."[100]

Meanwhile Sir Rowland Hill in his retirement was writing in his journal: "I must own that I am not very sorry to learn that the conspirators against me are now quarrelling as to the division of the spoil. There has, I learn, been a fearful passage of arms between Trollope and Tilley—Trollope, of course, being the aggressor."[101]

Scudamore's principal achievement in the Post Office was the taking over of private telegraph companies and making that service part of the Post Office monopoly. In 1874, describing the way in which Marie Melmotte's elopement was intercepted with the help of a telegram, Trollope wrote in *The Way We Live Now* (chap. 50), "It may be well doubted whether upon the whole the telegraph has not added more to the annoyances than to the comforts of life. . . . Poor Marie, when she heard her fate, would certainly have gladly hanged Mr. Scudamore."

Retirement from the Post Office

 The Post Office committee of 1860–61, of which Trollope had been a member, did not take up in any detail the organization of the London postal system, but it did recommend that more

high administrative staff was needed in the Circulation
Department, which was the branch that handled the distribution of letters within the metropolitan area. In 1856
London had been divided into postal districts for the
sorting and delivery of mail; despite the ridicule of the
Times in 1860 that letters marked "N.W." and "S.W."
were sent to North Wales and South Wales, Tilley could
affirm that during the day a letter would be delivered
within an hour if it was addressed to the same postal
district in which it was deposited.[102] (There were then
about a dozen collections and deliveries in a day.) Nevertheless, the task of supervision was too great for the
single controller of the Circulation Department, and
Tilley in late March, 1866, informed the postmaster
general that he was eager to make eight of the ten metropolitan postal districts (excluding West Central and
East Central, the area around the General Post Office
itself, which would continue as they were) each into a
separate "post town" under its own postmaster, and all
under a newly created surveyor, on analogy with post
towns in the rest of England. In order to examine into
the feasibility of the scheme, he asked for authority to
appoint some competent person to draw up a report.
The competent person was Trollope.[103]

The report itself was submitted with a speed that
clearly shows the move was a foregone conclusion: on
May 9 Tilley was able to say that Trollope had fur-
nished "abundant evidence of the advantages to be
gained by the change." By June 15 the scheme was in
effect and Trollope had been assigned the temporary
surveyorship, as well as direct responsibility (function-
ing as "postmaster") for the Western and the North
Eastern districts of London. His headquarters were fit-

ted out in the Vere Street post office, just off Oxford
Street and near Cavendish Square.

The transition was by no means easy. One of the
most difficult problems was the reassignment of all the
staff in such a way that the altered needs of the new
arrangement would not jeopardize their seniority; in
the end, most of the old staff retained their old titles,
though inappropriate to the new structure. Trollope
worked with his customary energy. Question after
question was resolved in written reports, and at the
same time he attended to such details as the inspection
of the physical aspects of the district post offices. (In
one of them he found the water closets and urinals
objectionably near to the windows of the kitchens in the
basement and requested £40 to provide the necessary
alterations.) One gets the impression that he went
about his business with an irresistible force: if he contravened an order from above, or neglected the sensi-
bilities of his colleagues, he brushed the offense aside
with a "So sorry!" and continued on his way.[104]

On June 20 Tilley offered him the permanent surveyorship of the Metropolitan District, at a salary which
would in the first year be the same as his current salary
of £700, but which because of the arduous nature of
the task would rise in four years to £800; the normal
maximum for surveyors was still £700. Trollope instantly declined with thanks, it may be supposed somewhat to Tilley's surprise. By August 8 he returned to
his district, accompanied by an expression of appreciation from the postmaster general "for the Services
which he has rendered to the Department in carrying
to a successful issue a difficult arrangement which involved no little labour and contrivance" (the words

were Tilley's; after all, the Duke of Montrose became postmaster general only in July).[105]

Trollope must have made clear to Tilley his reasons for declining the new appointment, but the explanation does not seem to have survived. One might speculate that he already had his resignation from the service in mind: even if it were only a faint idea, he would be abandoning the option if he took on a new and very important responsibility. (Edmund Yates commented that toward the end of his Post Office career, Trollope's involvements in literature had become more strenuous, his interest in the service less overwhelming.)[106] Or perhaps he simply felt comfortable in his way of life at Waltham Cross. His own district had been expanded somewhat by the addition of the area around Peterborough in a rearrangement of surveyors' districts he had helped to define earlier in 1866. Under this arrangement his seventy-seven post towns were the largest number in any district, though the average weekly circulation in it of 747,336 letters was sixth of the ten.[107]

A little over a year later he made up his mind. On October 4, 1867, Tilley forwarded Trollope's resignation from the service to the Duke of Montrose, with a long letter outlining the terms in which the Duke might wish to express his appreciation of Trollope's faithful and energetic work for the department. The Duke took his cue, and six days later Tilley could forward Trollope's response: "You will be glad to see that Mr. Trollope is pleased with his letter." Indeed he was: he copied it verbatim into *An Autobiography,* with only the very slightest suggestion of irony that shows his awareness of the personal relationship between the author of the letter and himself. Tilley had secured the Duke's endorsement of the proposition that "in spite of the many calls upon his time Mr. Trollope has never permitted his other avocations to interfere with his Post Office work which has always been faithfully and indeed energetically performed." In resigning he gave up all claim to a pension, for which indeed he would have had to work another eight years (to age sixty) and which would then in any case have amounted to a mere £500 a year or less. He had already laid aside enough of his literary earnings to produce such an income, and the freedom from postal duties enabled him to accept the editorship of *St. Pauls Magazine* at £1000 a year, one quarter of which went to pay his assistant, Edward Dicey. Almost his last official act was to resist attempts to cut down early morning deliveries and reduce salaries in suburban towns in his district.[108] His post was taken over by Charles Rea, who had deputized for him more than once during leaves of absence and duties elsewhere.

A decade after Trollope's death his contemporary at the Post Office, Edmund Yates—a man notorious for his literary quarrels and for conducting a weekly journal (the *World*) Trollope may have had in mind when he described the gossip sheet *Everybody's Business* in *Dr. Wortle's School*—wrote in that journal:

> A man with worse or more offensive manners than Trollope I have rarely met. He was coarse, boorish, rough, noisy, overbearing, insolent; he adopted the Johnsonian tactics of trying to outroar his adversary in argument; he sputtered and shouted, and glared through his spectacles, and waved his arms about, a sight for gods and men. . . . By the officials who were subordinate to him . . . he was pretty generally hated for the particularly objectionable manner in which he treated them. . . . I have heard of several instances,

[however,] and I know of one, to prove that he had a
kind heart.[109]

The records of the Post Office reveal the quarrelsome-
ness and the occasional bullying; they also reveal a man
who on principle worked hard for the well-being of all
civil servants, not merely himself, and whose intelligent
energy in the interest of the Post Office is not easily
matched.

A farewell dinner was given for Trollope by his colleagues on the evening of Thursday, October 31, at the
Albion Tavern, with Scudamore in the chair and Yates
as vice chairman. Tilley was of course present. "The
toast of the evening was very cleverly proposed by Mr.
Scudamore, and that of the visitors, very facetiously by
Mr. Edmund Yates, and a very successful evening was
spent," reported the *Times*. It was a much more quiet
occasion than the grand public dinner given for Dickens two days later on his departure for America (at
which Trollope was a speaker).[110]

For the first time in nearly thirty-three years Trollope was not a civil servant. When Tilley in 1878 became discouraged with his own work in the Post Office
and asked Trollope's advice on whether he should re-
tire (since his pension would be as large as his salary),
Trollope replied:

> A man who works for his bread is so much nobler than
> he who takes his bread for nothing. . . . You say of
> me:—that I would not choose to write novels unless I
> were paid. Most certainly I would;—much rather than
> not write them at all. The two points to be looked at
> are, your happiness,—(provided that the happiness of
> others dependent on you is indifferent in the matter,—)
> and your duty. What future employment do you pro-
> pose for yourself? In some respects you have limited

yourself more clearly than many men. You cannot stand in a club window; you cannot play cards; you cannot farm. Books must be your resource. I hardly know whether you can be happy four hours at a spell with a book. I do know that such happiness comes only from practice, and that the habit will not be acquired late in life. As to duty I am convinced that you ought to go if you believe it to be better for the service that you should do so;—or to remain for the same reason. . . . If it be that weariness tends to make your work unserviceable, I think you should go. If there be no such conviction, I think that for your own sake you should remain another term. Your happiness is so much to me that I cannot but write about it much in earnest.

Tilley remained in the service another two years, then retired upon the death of his third wife and was knighted on the occasion.[111]

The Mission to America

On June 18, 1867, a postal convention between England and the United States was signed in London to replace the convention of 1848. The chief British negotiator was Sir Rowland Hill's brother Frederic, as supervisor of the mail packet service. Frederic Hill was an ardent advocate of the doctrines of "political economy," a free trader of the Manchester school. And so he willingly acceded to the American views which left each country free to fix its own rates for international mail (below a specified maximum rate agreed upon) and to ship its mails by whatever vessels it found least expensive. How Tilley was lulled into accepting the agreement is not clear.

For in so agreeing, Hill knowingly went counter to Tilley's doctrine of the primacy of speed and efficiency, which he conceived would be best achieved by long-term contracts with a single packet company operating over the most direct route—in this case Cunard between New York and Queenstown—on a schedule fixed by the Post Office and with strict provision for penalties in case of tardiness. But Cunard declined to bid on a contract that gave them the mails in one direction only, and the United States was keeping its end open, partly at least with a view to using mail contracts in future to subsidize American ships. And so only six months after the convention was signed, the British Post Office gave the required twelve months notice that it would terminate the agreement on December 31, 1868, and wished to reopen negotiations.[112]

"It will be necessary to send a strong man," wrote Tilley to the Duke of Montrose on December 12, 1867, "and I think of proposing to you to ask Mr. Trollope to undertake the revision as we shall get the benefit not only of his ability but of his personal popularity with the Americans. I know of no one else who would do the work so well."[113] Trollope accepted the commission formally on February 29 (informally of course he had accepted it some weeks before that), and by way of giving dignity to the mission was presented at the Prince of Wales's levee on March 17. He was given his instructions on April 9 with full assurance that whatever he agreed to within their framework would be accepted, and sailed from Liverpool on April 11. The pay was five guineas per diem plus passage and actual expenses. It was a chance to earn extra money, to visit a country he liked, and to see old friends; no doubt the business with *St. Pauls* could be put sufficiently in order and in any case he would not be gone long. But that sailing was the beginning of a miserable quarter of a year.

In the first place, when Trollope reached Washington on the twenty-fourth, the impeachment trial of President Johnson was occupying the attention of Congress and the uncertainty of the verdict made the tenure in office of the American postmaster general, Alexander W. Randall, also uncertain; he declined to deal with Trollope until the trial was over. And so Trollope went off to Boston from May 6 to 15. Johnson was acquitted on Saturday, May 16, and Randall and his senior clerk, Joseph H. Blackfan, superintendent of foreign mails (for whom Trollope formed a high regard as "the man who really understands the question") gave over the whole of the following Monday to Trollope, but only so that they could make clear to him that they would not bind themselves to a regular schedule of ships or a manner of payment in harmony with the British. " 'Do you do as you like, and let us do as we like.' That is their argument; and that, they say—no doubt with truth—, was our argument also when the last convention was a making." (Randall even quoted at length a letter from Frederic Hill written during the previous negotiation, in support of his position.) Randall, moreover, was perfectly content to do without a postal agreement between the two countries, if it came to that. Trollope suspected that the German steamship lines (which called at Southampton, but not Queenstown) had him in their pocket, but it is clear that American shipping interests were also involved.

In view of the impasse, Tilley on June 8 urged the British Treasury—which had to approve the negotiations—to let Trollope simply make the best deal he could. "It is not desirable to detain Mr. Trollope in America longer than is absolutely necessary." There was no reply; meanwhile Trollope was getting restless, for he could not leave Washington, and a city which in April and May is delightful grows unbearable in late June. "Take pity on Trollope and let us have an answer," Tilley urged the Treasury on June 17, and again on June 27: "Might I ask you . . . to come to a decision as to the American postal convention. . . . Trollope went out to please me at some inconvenience to himself and he is most anxious to get back."[114] Trollope, sadly, was writing his epitaph:

> Washington has slain this man,
> By politics and heat together.
> Sumner alone he might have stood
> But not the Summer weather.

"This place is so awful to me, that I doubt whether I can stand it much longer. To make matters worse a democratic Senator who is stone deaf and who lives in the same house with me [Wormley's, on I Street], has proposed to dine with me every day! I refused three times but he did not hear me, and ordered that our dinners should be served together. I had not the courage to fight it any further, and can see no alternative but to run away." A decade later he still remembered that "in June the musquito of Washington is as a roaring lion."[115] He could allow himself only brief excursions, to Richmond and Baltimore in May and to New York in June; even the last was cut short by a cable from London. He saw almost none of his American friends. He wrote desperately to Scudamore for another thousand dollars. At last the telegram went out to him on July 1: "Make Treaty on the best terms you can."

The terms were indeed bad ones. Trollope forwarded two newspaper clippings to support his view
that "the motive power in all this is the influence of
certain members of Congress who know and care nothing for the transit of mails, but who do know and care a
great deal about certain Companies." One of these was a
leading article from the Washington *Morning Chronicle*
of July 2: "That [former] treaty secured important advantages in the reduction of the rates of postage, but the
wiseacre who controls the British Postal Department in
the interest of a subsidized line of steamers" has canceled it and proposes that all mails both ways be carried
on British ships. "This is a very pretty little plan, and
Mr. Anthony Trollope has come over here . . . for the
purpose of negotiating an arrangement whereby it may
be carried into practical effect." He was obliged to get
authorization for further retreats from the British position. Then Randall went off to the Democratic national
convention in New York, leaving Trollope to endure the
heat of Washington a few days longer.

"I cannot but feel that they have had the whip hand
of us altogether," he wrote. The treaty he concluded on
July 11 settled almost nothing except an agreed rate of
postage per letter of twelve cents or sixpence and a
provision that each country might keep whatever fines
it collected for insufficient prepaid postage instead of
having to account to the other country. Trollope
rushed to New York on the twelfth, spent a night in
Boston, and sailed from New York on the fifteenth.[116]
Even the cool spray of Niagara Falls was denied him.
He reached home on the twenty-sixth, to conclude a
mission of one hundred and eleven days, for which he
received £582 15s. and a message of thanks from the
Duke of Montrose, who regarded the mission as a fail-

ure but was "satisfied that no exertions on [Trollope's] part were spared to attain the end in view."

There was a lapse of several years before he could use his experience with American legislators in a novel about *The American Senator* (not the deaf one he knew), or add his American lecturer, Olivia Q. Fleabody (*Is He Popenjoy?*) to those he fancied surrounding Kate Field in America—"Janet L. Tozer, Annie B. Slocum, Martha M. Mumpus, Violet Q. Fitzpopam etc."[117]

He also had carried with him to America, at his own request, a commission from the Foreign Office to make an effort to secure an international copyright agreement between the United States and Great Britain. There is obviously no record of this aspect of his mission in the Post Office archives. It bore no fruit, but it did lead to his membership in the Copyright Commission of 1876 (likewise a fruitless enterprise).[118]

The Beverley Election

By what may seem to be a peculiarity of the election laws, Trollope for most of his life was ineligible to vote for a member of Parliament: many civil servants, like lunatics, lords, and of course women, were without the franchise.[119] His political preferences, however, were not secret; his closest friends were Liberals. There was of course political business in some of Trollope's earlier novels, including the campaigning in *Doctor Thorne*, but the first detailed examination of an election was that of George Vavasor in *Can You Forgive Her?* (1864), the first novel of the "parliamentary" series, where the frustration and ruinous expense of winning a bye-election, only to lose the seat almost immediately through a dissolution of Parliament, drove Vavasor out of his mind. Vavasor is the villain of the novel, but Trollope makes us sympathize with the force of his desperation.

Again and again in his novels he had expressed the view that the highest honor to which an Englishman might aspire was the privilege of passing through the Members' entrance to the House of Commons. From the moment of his retirement from the Post Office, therefore, Trollope not surprisingly looked about him for an opportunity to sit in the House. He was at first urged by Andrew Johnston, one of the leading Liberals of the county, to stand for South Essex, the prevailingly Liberal district near which he resided; then Johnston changed his mind, stood himself, and what looked like a sure seat for Trollope disappeared.[120] Where the suggestion came from that he stand for the Yorkshire borough of Beverley is not clear—presumably from Liberal party offices. But candidacy in Beverley was quite a different matter and the service required of a Liberal candidate there was not to win, which was impossible, but to let the Conservatives show their hand and disqualify themselves (under newly revised statutes) by corruption. The population of Beverley was about twelve thousand, of whom somewhat over two thousand were registered electors. The number was barely enough to escape the provisions of the new distribution of seats in 1867, and the borough continued to send two members to Parliament. The Conservative candidates in 1868 were Sir Henry Edwards, one of the directors of a local factory who had represented the borough since August, 1857, and Captain Edmund H. Kennard, a new man and an outsider looking for a

sure seat. Trollope's colleague on the Liberal side was
the Hon. Marmaduke Constable Maxwell, son of the
Earl Herries, who lived near Beverley.[121]

Trollope's agents distributed his printed election address, dated October 28, 1868; he appeared in person
before the voters on October 30 and again on November 9, 11, 12, 13, and 16.[122] At some time during the
campaign he also sat on the platform at a crowded
meeting in St. James's Hall, Regent Street, in support
of the candidacy of John Stuart Mill for reelection for
Westminster (the seat that Melmotte later won in *The
Way We Live Now*), and the clear, ringing accents of his
short and forcible speech were said to have contrasted
most strikingly with the candidate's voice, which could
scarcely be heard by those nearest to him.[123] If the newspaper reports from Beverley make his speeches sound
tepid, they were at least intelligent and to the point.
One of the issues to which he addressed himself was
the long overdue provision of elementary education for
all the people (a promise the Liberals fulfilled with
Forster's Elementary Education Act of 1870); another
was the disestablishment of the Anglican Church of
Ireland, which came in 1869. He had to skirt the issue
of the secret ballot, which the Liberals advocated as a
guard against corruption and which Trollope himself
disliked as unmanly. The election of 1868 was in fact
the last general election conducted by open voting. In
general he seemed to rest on the self-evident proposition that the populace of an industrial town had far
more to expect from the Liberals than from the Conservatives. He ignored the immediate cash benefits the
Conservatives were paying to the voters. Trollope was
of course present on the day of the election, November
17. Up until about eleven o'clock he and Maxwell were

still leading, but at the close of the polls it was announced that Edwards received 1132 votes, Kennard 986, Maxwell 895, and Trollope 740. Maxwell's margin over Trollope may be attributable to his being a local man. (Since each elector had two votes, more than 39 percent of the electors voted for Trollope.) Speaking from the hustings when the poll was announced, he said: "It may be that I shall appear before you again, and if I do I shall hope that you will think I have done nothing to forfeit your friendship." His formal farewell address dated from Waltham Cross the next day expressed the same hope. According to the Liberal *Beverley Recorder* Trollope and Maxwell were greeted by the crowd with an ovation that seemed to belie the announcement of their defeat then being made.

But Beverley had sent its last members to Parliament. The local Liberal committee immediately filed a petition charging corruption and asking that the election be set aside. The case was heard before Sir Samuel Martin, a Baron of Exchequer, on March 9–11, 1869; 109 witnesses testified (Trollope was not among them), and at the conclusion Martin announced that he would report to the Speaker of the House "that, in his opinion, this election was void at common law; that a very large number of the electors of this borough were bribed and did sell their votes under the influence of bribery" (Martin estimated the number at more than 800), and—most important of all—that he felt obliged to make a special report on the matter to the attorney general.[124] A commission of three lawyers was set up by the government, which in thirty-eight days of hearings from August 24 to November 17 examined over 700 witnesses. Trollope appeared before them in Beverley on September 3. Much of the testimony was devoted to the municipal

election at Beverley only fifteen days before the parliamentary election, and it was established that by general
consent in the community a bribe accepted in the
former was held to include payment for a vote in the
latter. The commission reported on January 29, 1870,
that corrupt practices had prevailed in Beverley at both
parliamentary elections in 1857, in 1859, 1860, 1865,
and 1868; it appended a list of over 600 persons (including both Edwards and Kennard) guilty of corruption at
one or more of these elections. (Edwards's margin of
victory over Trollope was less than 400.) Trollope and
his colleague were not under suspicion. The government prepared, and Parliament passed, a bill depriving
Beverley of its parliamentary representation (hencefor-
ward its voters would help elect the member for the East
Riding of Yorkshire), and permanently disfranchising
all those listed by the commission as bribers or bribed.[125]

The cost to Trollope was about £400 plus a share in
the actual expense of holding the election, including
beer for the officers at the polls; the entire amount was
about £440.[126] There is no evidence that any of the
expenses of the proceedings subsequent to the election
fell on him, since he was not one of the petitioners. He
had done good service for his party; if he did not help
them to secure two Liberal voices behind the Treasury
bench, he at least helped them get rid of two Conservative voices on the other side. More interesting to him
than the practical aspect was his conviction that he had
struck a successful blow against the degradation of elec-
toral corruption. And whatever illusions he may have
allowed himself during the campaign, he must have
known (and indeed on his own testimony he had been
told in advance) that this was the service he had been
sent to perform.[127] Nevertheless, what he really wanted

was a seat in Parliament; "I shall have another fly at it somewhere some day, unless I feel myself to be growing too old," he told a friend.[128] But by the next general election (1874) he was fifty-nine. His novels continued to express his sense that such a seat is the highest position to which an Englishman may aspire. Dickens, who had declined an invitation to stand for Birmingham in that election of 1868, did not agree: "The House of Commons . . . is a dismal sight. . . . Its irrationality and dishonesty are quite shocking. . . . Anthony's ambition [at Beverley] is inscrutable to me. Still, it is the ambition of many men; and the honester the man who entertains it, the better for the rest of us, I suppose."[129]

"What an idea does [Cicero] give as to the labour of a candidate in Rome!" Trollope wrote in 1880. "I can imagine it to be worse even than the canvassing of an English borough, which to a man of spirit and honour is the most degrading of all existing employments not held to be absolutely disgraceful."[130] But this much contact with public life had been profitable to Trollope, not only in the strong political sense it gave his novels, but in his vivid perception of the political careers of Cicero and Palmerston, whose lives he published in 1880 and 1882.

After Retirement

John Tilley occasionally passed on to Trollope in his retirement news of his friends in the service, and Trollope once forwarded for Tilley's stern attention a letter that had taken forty-eight hours to reach him after posting in London: the posts must be kept up to standard![131] In 1871 he gave up the house at Waltham Cross from which he had administered his surveyor's district and nearly two years later took a lease on Number 39, Montagu Square, in the parish in which his sister had been married; his good friend Sir Frederick Pollock lived in that square and the location was both convenient and attractive (a plaque now commemorates his residence there). He traveled twice to Australia (where his younger son Fred lived), both times returning across the United States, and once to South Africa; the immediate fruits of these journeys were his *Australia and New Zealand* and *South Africa.* "Wherever I go I visit the post-office, feeling certain that I may be able to give a little good advice. Having looked after post-offices for thirty years at home I fancy that I could do very good service among the Colonies if I could have arbitrary power given to me to make what changes I pleased. My advice is always received with attention and respect, and I have generally been able to flatter myself that I have convinced my auditors. But I never knew an instance yet in which any improvement recommended by me was carried out," he wrote in 1878. Even during a three-hour stop under the midnight sun in the tiny Faroe Islands, he wanted to question the postmaster about his duties, about the closeness of supervision from Denmark, about the splendor of his uniform.[132]

His novels also reflected these travels. *Harry Heathcote of Gangoil* was set in Australia after the first journey, *John Caldigate* had important Australian scenes after the second. Some scenes of *Dr. Wortle's School* draw upon his journey homeward across the United States, and the South African gold fields figure in *An Old Man's Love.*

The story of *John Caldigate* is a piece of detective fiction that depends on the evidence of a letter that purported to have passed through the Australian mails. Caldigate had been living intimately with a presumed widow, Mrs. Euphemia Smith, in the rough Australian mining town of Ahalala, near Nobble; he had never married her, but after his return to England and his marriage to Hester Bolton she and some confederates followed him and, failing in blackmail, brought charges of bigamy against him. Mrs. Smith was able to produce an envelope undoubtedly addressed in Caldigate's hand to "Mrs. Caldigate" at Ahalala. Caldigate claimed he had merely written the direction on the envelope in a sentimental moment while they were living together, and had then tossed it aside, but the woman affirmed that he had sent it to her with a letter while he was away at Sydney and that it constituted a clear and public acknowledgment that he regarded her as his wife. The envelope indeed bore a twopenny postage stamp of New South Wales and a clear Sydney postmark of May 10, 1873—that time a few years earlier when they had been together in the gold fields. It should also have been postmarked on arrival at Nobble, and was not, but the omission was not material since irregularities might be expected in a remote post town. Various attempts to discredit the postmark failed: there could be no doubt that it had been stamped on the envelope in the Sydney post office. A clerk from the General Post Office in London, Samuel Bagwax, whose specialty in St. Martin's-le-Grand was date-stamping letters, was called upon to testify at the trial, and though convinced that there had been fraud he was at loss to find evidence. He continued to study the matter after Caldigate's conviction and imprisonment. Post Office regulations required that the Sydney post office keep daily impressions of all the date stamps used—perhaps these might show minute deviations that would prove the date stamp on the letter fraudulent. And then a new idea struck him. As every stamp collector knows, English nineteenth-century postage stamps bear in their corners mysterious letters of the alphabet in curious combinations; the postage stamp on the incriminating letter carried a *P* in each lower corner, and Bagwax learned that stamps with *P*s in the lower corners were not printed before 1874—therefore the letter could not have passed through the mails in 1873 and the date stamp had been falsified in the Sydney post office at a later date! Caldigate was released by special pardon from the Home Secretary. In a footnote Trollope apologized to his "friends in the Sydney post-office" for this account; "I know how well the duties are done in that office."[133]

A few years after Trollope's retirement, a new building was erected opposite the building in which he had served his apprenticeship in St. Martin's-le-Grand, in order to house the recently acquired telegraphic operations. He paid the new building a visit early in 1877 and described for the public his pleasure in the industry and competence of "The Young Women at the London Telegraph Office"; he had nothing but praise for this new departure from the masculine civil service he had known, and soon afterward wrote a short story on "The Telegraph Girl."[134]

Trollope keeps himself very much in his novels, from the literary man at the hunting meet at Edgehill who had done his three hours' writing by candlelight before journeying down to the hunt (*Can You Forgive Her?* chap. 17) to the dinner guest who sopped up on a napkin after every spoonful the soup he had dripped on his beard, "as men with beards always do" (*Doctor Thorne,* chap. 35) and the praise of the discoverer of a reducing diet, "that great Banting who has preserved us all so completely from the horrors of obesity" (*The Fixed Period,* chap. 9). Novel after novel shows his pride in the Post Office, his knowledge of its practices, his amusement at the eccentricities of its patrons. Mr. Somers's letter left county Cork after Herbert Fitzgerald's departure but reached London before him, "having been conveyed with that lightning rapidity for which the British Post-office has ever been remarkable—and especially that portion of it which has reference to the sister island" (*Castle Richmond,* chap. 37). Mr. Caldigate calculated nicely the time of the mails from New South Wales, which he knew came *via* San Francisco; Mrs. Masters could almost, but not quite, persuade the obliging local postmaster to surrender to her, in violation of regulations, the letter Mary Masters had put in the post for Larry Twentyman, for the postmaster "had been thoroughly grounded in his duties by one of those trusty guardians of our correspondence who inspect and survey our provincial post offices" (*John Caldigate,* chap. 13; *The American Senator,* chap. 34). Rachel Ray's mother thought money orders were "so very convenient,—that is if you've got the money"; Mr. Burton wished there were no such thing as the penny post, since now people expected one to write so many more letters (*Rachel Ray,* chap. 19; *The Claverings,* chap. 26). Lady Laura's letter was delivered to Phineas Finn on the very afternoon of the day it was written, "having reached London by same day mail from Glasgow" (*Phineas Finn,* chap. 53). (Trollope had spent some weeks in Glasgow in May–June, 1865, reorganizing the posts, and one of his tasks was to

speed up the service to London.)[135] The vicar of Bullhampton "carried on a perpetual feud with the Post-
office authorities" because his village "unfortunately was
at the end of the postman's walk, and as the man came
all the way from Lavington, letters were seldom received
much before eleven o'clock." It was the vicar's "great
postal doctrine that letters ought to be rained from
heaven on to everybody's breakfast-table exactly as the
hot water is brought in for tea," and "being an energetic
man, [he] carried on a long and angry correspondence
with the authorities aforesaid" (*Vicar of Bullhampton*,
chap. 22). More seriously, Trollope challenged the con-
ventional notion that the civil servants were notoriously
lax in performing their tasks:

> The popular newspaper, the popular member of Par-
> liament, and the popular novelist—the name of Charles
> Dickens will of course present itself to the reader who
> remembers the Circumlocution office [in *Little Dorrit*],—
> have had it impressed on their several minds,—and
> have endeavoured to impress the same idea on the
> minds of the public generally,—that the normal Gov-
> ernment clerk is quite indifferent to his work. No
> greater mistake was ever made, or one showing less
> observation of human nature. It is the nature of a man
> to appreciate his own work. . . . The fault lies on the
> other side. The policeman is ambitious of arresting
> everybody. The lawyer would rather make your will for
> you gratis than let you make your own. . . . Curlydown
> [a colleague of Bagwax] would willingly have expended
> the whole net revenue of the post-office—and his
> own,—in improving the machinery for stamping let-
> ters. [*John Caldigate*, chap. 47]

The passage is an echo of one in the earliest version of
The Three Clerks two decades earlier.[136]

These are no doubt rather trivial aspects of Trollope's work. Far more significant is the range of knowledge of Ireland and England that his Post Office experience had given him. A sense of place dominates his novels, from the earliest and the very latest in Ireland to all those in England throughout the rest of his career. It is not the "regional" peculiarities (he seldom uses dialect, for example, in the English novels, and when he does so it is more commonly intended to show social level than regional distinctions), but simply the way a place looks, and there is hardly a part of England that his novels do not take us to. Often the place-names are perfectly straightforward and real; when they are fictitious, we feel tempted to believe that our maps are at fault. If the postman's walk goes from Lavington to Bullhampton, why should Lavington be on our map and Bullhampton not?

He was even more sensitive to the geography of London than to that of the provinces. People live precisely where they ought to live and under the circumstances they would find there.[137] Private hotels like that in which Johnny Eames lived on Burton Crescent (now Cartwright Gardens) are well known to students who work in the British Museum. The barrister Furnival's success is measured by the progress of his homes westward in London from his beginnings in Keppel Street, where another barrister had become the father of Anthony Trollope in 1815; despite the increasing luxury, Mrs. Furnival almost thought her happiest days had been spent in Keppel Street (*Orley Farm*, chap. 10). Bayswater with its Porchester Gardens and Terrace has exactly the right tone for Mrs. Dobbs Broughton and her friend Lady Demolines (*Last Chronicle of Barset*). Trollope's occasional blunders then are the more surprising, and none more surprising than one that occupies the center of the stage in *Can You Forgive Her?* (chap. 66). Lady Monk, Burgo Fitzgerald's aunt, has a large house appropriately enough on Gloucester Square, north of Hyde Park, where she gives a large party from which Burgo plans to elope with Lady Glencora Palliser. But the elopement does not take place; Glencora returns home to Park Lane with her husband, and Burgo wanders the streets alone. Suddenly one discovers that Lady Monk's house has moved to Grosvenor Square, not by a mere slip of the pen, but by the whole pattern of Burgo's walk, first to dismiss the carriage that has been waiting for him and Lady Glencora "in Bruton Street, some five minutes' walk from his aunt's house" (Bruton Street runs into Berkeley Square, close to Grosvenor Square), then down Park Street and through a mews to Park Lane, over Park Lane to Oxford Street, along to Bond Street, and then back to the house in Grosvenor Square!

Trollope gave up his home in Montagu Square in 1880 and moved to the country once more—to Harting, near Petersfield, just inside Hampshire from the border of Surrey, where a distant cousin had once been vicar.[138] It was an ill-fated move; he was too old to travel to town as much as he had to do and the climate troubled him severely. Two short final journeys to Ireland with his niece Florence Bland in the spring and summer of 1882 to provide a background for *The Landleaguers* were enlivened by meetings with old friends in the Irish Post Office and recollections of pleasant days in Clonmel and elsewhere. In September, 1882, he and his wife took for the winter a suite of rooms in Garlant's Hotel at the top of Suffolk Street, Pall Mall (immediately behind the Haymarket Theatre); it was the hotel in which Mrs. Arabin (*Last Chronicle*, chap. 70) and the Dean of Brotherton (*Is He Popenjoy?* chap. 26) were accustomed to stay.

At the home of Sir John Tilley after dinner on November 3, 1882, Trollope was smitten with the fatal stroke from which he never fully recovered consciousness. He died on December 6 in a nursing home at 34 Welbeck Street, less than a quarter of a mile from the Northumberland Street lodgings in which he had lived as a junior clerk in the Post Office.

Appendixes

Appendix 1

Trollope on the Civil Service

1. "The Civil Service," *Dublin University Magazine* 46 (October, 1855): 409–26. Anonymous. On "Papers Relating to the Reorganization of the Civil Service, Presented to Parliament by Command of Her Majesty" (commonly known as the "Northcote/Trevelyan Report").
2. An "article on the 3rd No of *Little Dorrit*" which Trollope sent to the editor of the *Athenaeum* from Dublin on February 5, 1856. The article was not published and apparently has not survived. The third number of *Little Dorrit* (chaps. 9–11) introduces the Circumlocution Office. See Bradford A. Booth, "Trollope and 'Little Dorrit,' " *The Trollopian* 2, (March, 1948): 237–40.
3. *The Three Clerks*. London, 1858. Vol. 2, chap. 12, pp. 251–75, "The Civil Service." This essay, which contains no reference to the novel in which it was embedded, was dropped from all editions subsequent to the first. It followed what is chap. 27 ("Excelsior") in the current editions.

   The Three Clerks was published in late November, 1857, and deals with three young civil servants. Of the administrators portrayed, Sir Gregory Hardlines is meant to suggest Sir Charles Trevelyan and the name of Sir Warwick Westend to suggest that of Sir Stafford Northcote.
4. "A speech which [Trollope] delivered at a meeting held at St. Martin's-le-Grand in 1858, to establish a Post Office Library and Literary Institution" was quoted in Edmund Yates, *Recollections and Experiences* (London: Bentley,

1884), 2:229–30. *The Times* of November 25, 1858, p. 10, col. 3 announced that at a meeting held "recently" at the Post Office, it had been resolved to establish a Post Office Library and Reading Room; no speeches were reported. Trollope was in London from November 3–16, 1858, and had been there also from May 10–25. This is apparently not the same speech as item 6.

5. "Report of the Select Committee on Civil Service Appointments, together with . . . Minutes of Evidence. Printed 9 July 1860." House of Commons, *Sessional Papers*, 1860, vol. 9; 158–80. Trollope and John Tilley appeared together as witnesses on Thursday, April 26. Most of the testimony was Tilley's. For comments by the civil service commissioners, see *Sessional Papers*, 1861, vol. 19: 529–33.

6a. Anthony Trollope, *Four Lectures*, ed. Morris L. Parrish (London: Constable, 1938), pp. 4–26 ("The Civil Service as a Profession"). Trollope delivered this paper as a lecture at the General Post Office in London on January 4, 1861, and had a copy printed from his manuscript in order to make his delivery the easier; Parrish prints from this lecture copy. The speech was reported in the newspapers—among others, the *Daily Telegraph* (London), Saturday, January 5, 1861, p. 3, cols. 1–2 (see also January 7, p. 4, cols. 4–5 and January 24, p. 5, col. 6); *Daily News* (London), January 5, 1861, p. 5, cols. 5–6; *Morning Post* (London), January 5, p. 6, cols. 3–4.

6b. "The Civil Service as a Profession," *Cornhill Magazine* 3 (February, 1861): 214–28. Unsigned. This version varies only slightly from the preceding, where the requirements of a periodical essay differ from those of a direct address to a body of civil servants.

7. *The Small House at Allington, Cornhill Magazine* 6–9 (September, 1862–April, 1864); in two volumes, March 17, 1864. Both John Eames and Adolphus Crosbie in this novel are civil servants, and the former's superior, Sir Raffle Buffle, necessarily embodies the essential characteristics of the higher civil servants as Trollope knew them. He "was intended to represent a type, not a man; but the man for the picture was soon chosen, and I was often assured that the portrait was very like. I have never

seen the gentleman with whom I am supposed to have taken the liberty."—*An Autobiography*, ed. Frederick Page (London: Oxford University Press, 1950), p. 179.

8. *North America.* London, 1862. Vol. 2, chap. 13, pp. 367–89, "The Post-Office."

9. "Usurers and Clerks in Public Offices," *Pall Mall Gazette* (London), March 23, 1865, p. 2. Anonymous.

10. "The Civil Service Commissioners," *Pall Mall Gazette* (London), July 27, 1865, pp. 3–4. Signed "A Civil Servant of Thirty Years' Standing." A reply to an article of July 25 by "Jacob Omnium" [M. J. Higgins]. Tilley forwarded a copy of Trollope's article approvingly to the postmaster general, Lord Stanley of Alderley, on July 28.

11. "The Civil Service," *Fortnightly Review* 2 (October 15, 1865): 613–26. Signed. On the Tenth [Annual] Report of Her Majesty's Civil Service Commissioners, 1865.

12. "The Young Women at the London Telegraph Office," *Good Words* 18 (June, 1877): 377–84. Signed.

13. *John Caldigate, Blackwood's Edinburgh Magazine* 123–25 (April, 1878–June, 1879); in three volumes, late May, 1879. Bagwax and Curlydown are civil servants in the Post Office.

14. *Marion Fay, Graphic* 24–25 (December 3, 1881–June 3, 1882); in three volumes, May 15, 1882. Chapters 7 ("The Post Office"), 30 ("New Year's Day"), 57 ("Crocker's Distress"), 58 ("Dismissal. B.B."), 61 ("Crocker's Tale"): scenes in the clerks' room of the office of the secretary of the Post Office, Sir Boreas Bodkin.

Significant references to the Civil Service will of course also be found in Trollope's correspondence and in *An Autobiography*.

Appendix 2

Calendar of Trollope's Principal Literary Works, 1843–68

1843–45 *The Macdermots of Ballycloran* (novel in three volumes; ca. 198,000 words).

Begun September, 1843, completed July, 1845. Publishing agreement dated September 15, 1845; published about March 13, 1847.

Set in and near Carrick on Shannon, county Leitrim, in the Central Postal District of Ireland.

ca. 1846–48   *The Kellys and the O'Kellys, or, Landlords and Tenants. A Tale of Irish Life* (novel in three volumes; ca. 178,000 words).
Publishing agreement dated March 30, 1848; published about June 22.

Set largely in Dunmore, county Galway, in the Central Postal District of Ireland. The hero, Lord Ballindine, takes his title from a town in the same county.

1849–50   Seven letters on "Irish Distress" and "The Real State of Ireland," signed "A.T." In the *Examiner*, August 25, 1849; March 30, April 6, May 11, June 1, 8, and 15, 1850.

ca. 1848–49   *La Vendée. An Historical Romance* (novel in three volumes; ca. 177,500 words).
Publishing agreement dated February 15, 1850; published about May 4.

Set in late eighteenth-century France.

[1850]   Chapters on Dublin and county Kerry for a proposed *Murray's Handbook for Ireland*.
Never published and not now known.

1853–54   *The Warden* (novel in one volume; ca. 73,000 words).
Begun July 29, 1853. Publishing agreement dated October 24, 1854; published about January 5, 1855.

Set chiefly in "Barsetshire," a fictitious county in the southwest of England, combining some aspects of Wiltshire and Somerset.

1854–56 *The New Zealander* (chapters on English life and institutions; ca. 88,500 words).
Forwarded to publishers, March 27, 1855; rejected. Revised at least to May 1856.

1855–56 *Barchester Towers* (novel in three volumes; ca. 203,000 words).
About one third of first volume complete by February 17, 1855; resumed May 12, 1856, and completed early November. Publishing agreement dated February 5, 1857; published about May 8.

Set in "Barsetshire."

1857 *The Three Clerks* (novel in three volumes; ca. 217,500 words plus 6,200-word essay on "The Civil Service").
Written February 15–August 18, 1857. Publishing agreement dated October 15; published about November 26, 1857, with date "1858."

Set principally in London and suburban Hampton (Middlesex).

1857–58 *Doctor Thorne* (novel in three volumes; ca. 225,000 words).
Written October 20, 1857–March 31, 1858. Publishing agreement dated January 29, 1858; published about May 20.

Set principally in "Barsetshire."

1858–59 *The Bertrams* (novel in three volumes; ca. 223,000 words).
Written April 1, 1858, to January 17, 1859: "Begun in Egypt, and written on the Mediterranean—in Malta, Gibraltar, England, Ireland, Scotland, and finished in the West Indies." Publishing agreement not dated; published about March 8.

Set in London, Palestine, "Littlebath" (Cheltenham), Cairo, and Hampshire.

1859   *The West Indies and the Spanish Main* (travel book in one volume; ca. 125,000 words).
Begun January 25, 1859. Publishing agreements dated April 9 and July 14; published about October 29.

1857, 1861   *The Struggles of Brown, Jones, and Robinson* (novel in one volume; ca. 71,500 words).
Written August 24–September 7, 1857; June, 1858; June 23–August 3, ?1861. Publishing agreement dated July 6, 1860; published serially each month from August, 1861, to March, 1862, and as a book in New York about April or May, 1862; in London about December 17, 1870.

Set in London.

1859–60   *Castle Richmond* (novel in three volumes; ca. 207,000 words).
Written August 4–30, October 30–31, 1859; January 2–March 25, 1860. Publishing agreement dated August 2, 1859; published about May 10, 1860.

Set in county Cork, Ireland, during the famine of 1846–47.

1859–60   *Framley Parsonage* (novel in three volumes; ca. 215,500 words).
Written November 2–December 23, 1859; April 3–June 27, 1860. Publishing agreement dated November 3, 1859; published serially each month from January, 1860, to April, 1861, and as a book about April 6.

Set in "Barsetshire."

1860   *Tales of All Countries* (volume of eight short stories; ca. 80,000 words).
Publishing agreement for book dated September 11, 1860; published in periodicals, February, May, August, October, and November, 1860, and as a book about November 16, 1861.

Set in the French Pyrenees, in county Mayo (Ireland), in Seville, in Jamaica, in Saratoga Springs (New York), at

Antwerp and Brussels, in Cairo (Egypt), and at Le Puy, France.

1860–61   *Orley Farm* (novel in two volumes published separately; ca. 312,500 words).
Written July 4, 1860 to June 22, 1861. Publishing agreement dated July 3, 1860; published in monthly parts, March, 1861, to October, 1862, and the two volumes about December 3, 1861, and September 25, 1862.

Set in London, Essex (Trollope's post office district), and near Leeds in Yorkshire.

1860–61   *Tales of All Countries* Second series (volume of nine short stories; ca. 95,000 words).
Periodical publication agreements dated December 22, 1860 and April 12, 1861; published in periodicals in January–March, November–December, 1861, and as a book about February 7, 1863.

Set in Palestine, Rome, Devonshire, Lake Como, Costa Rica, Munich, Bermuda, Suez, and Liverpool.

1861–62   *North America* (travel book in two volumes; ca. 296,000 words).
Written September 16, 1861, to April 25, 1862. Publishing agreement dated March 20, 1861; published about May 19, 1862.

1862–63   *The Small House at Allington* (novel in two volumes; ca. 260,000 words).
Written May 20, 1862, to February 11, 1863. Publishing agreement dated July 6, 1861; published serially each month from September, 1862, to April, 1864, and as a book about March 17, 1864.

Set in "Barsetshire," London, and Baden-Baden.

1863   *Rachel Ray* (novel in two volumes; ca. 142,500 words).
Written March 3–June 29, 1863. Agreements for periodical publication (later abandoned) dated April 7 and De-

cember 5, 1862, and for book publication dated January 26 and June 10, 1863; published about October 12.

Set in the fictitious market town of "Baslehurst," on the River Avon.

1863–64 *Can You Forgive Her?* (novel in two volumes published separately; ca. 312,500 words).
Written August 16, 1863, to April 28, 1864. Publishing agreement dated January 26, 1863; published in monthly parts from January, 1864, to August, 1865, and the two volumes about September 29, 1864, and July 29, 1865.

Set in London, Cambridgeshire, Norfolk, Westmorland, and in Switzerland and elsewhere on the Continent.

1864 *Miss Mackenzie* (novel in two volumes; ca. 144,500 words).
Written May 22–August 18, 1864. Publishing agreement dated February 23, 1864; published about February 18, 1865.

Set in London and "Littlebath" (Cheltenham).

1864 *The Claverings* (novel in two volumes; ca. 206,500 words).
Written August 24–December 31, 1864. Publishing agreement dated November 13, 1863; published serially each month from February, 1866, to May, 1867, and as a book about April 20.

Set in "Clavering" (a parish in the diocese of "Barchester") and London.

1865 *Hunting Sketches* (volume of eight sketches; ca. 19,500 words).
Published serially February 9–March 20, 1865, and as a book about May 10.

1865 *The Belton Estate* (novel in three volumes; ca. 154,000 words).

Written January 30–September 4, 1865. Publishing agreements dated April 5 and May 5, 1865; published serially each fortnight from May 15, 1865, to January 1, 1866, and as a book about December 30, 1865.

Set in the west of England, London, Norfolk, and Yorkshire.

1865   *Travelling Sketches* (volume of eight sketches; ca. 18,000 words).
Published serially, August–September, 1865, and as a book about February 10, 1866.

1865   *Nina Balatka. The Story of a Maiden of Prague* (anonymous novel in two volumes; ca. 74,000 words).
Written November 3–December 31, 1865. Publishing agreement dated April 14, 1866; published serially each month from July, 1866, to January, 1867, and as a book about January 26.

Set in Prague.

1865–66   *Clergymen of the Church of England* (volume of ten sketches; ca. 26,000 words).
Published serially from November, 1865, to January, 1866, and as a book about March 29.

1866   *The Last Chronicle of Barset* (novel in two volumes published separately; ca. 346,000 words).
Written January 21–September 15, 1866. Publishing agreement dated February 6, 1866; published in weekly parts from December 1, 1866, to July 6, 1867, and the two volumes about March 14 and July 4, 1867.

Set in "Barsetshire" and London.

1861–67   *Lotta Schmidt and Other Stories* (volume of nine short stories, a third series of *Tales of All Countries;* ca. 79,000 words).
Published in collections or periodicals in November, 1861; January, March, and December, 1863; December, 1864;

May, July, and September, 1866; and January, 1867; and
as a book about August 24, 1867.

Set in Vienna; London and Manchester; Kentucky; "Bally-
moy," county Galway (Ireland); Cornwall; Cheshire; Ven-
ice and Verona; Boston, Massachusetts; on shipboard
from St. Thomas to Panama.

1866–67 *Phineas Finn, the Irish Member* (novel in two volumes, ca. 266,500 words).
Written November 17, 1866, to May 15, 1867. Publishing
agreement dated January 24, 1867; published serially each
month from October, 1867, to May, 1869, and as a book
about March 4, 1869.

Set in the west of Ireland, in London, in Scotland, and on
the coast of Belgium.

1867 *Linda Tressel* (anonymous novel in two volumes, ca.
70,000 words).
Written June 2–July 10, 1867. Publishing agreement
dated July 16; published serially each month from October, 1867, to May, 1868, and as a book about May 2.

Set in Nuremberg, Augsburg, and Cologne.

1867 *The Golden Lion of Granpere* (novel in one volume; ca.
66,500 words).
Written September 1–October 22, 1867. Publishing agreement dated April 14, 1871; published serially each month,
January–August, 1872, and as a book about April 24,
1872.

Set in Lorraine.

1867–68 *He Knew He Was Right* (novel in two volumes; ca.
340,000 words).
Written November 13, 1867 to June 12, 1868. Publishing
agreement dated November 15, 1867; published in both
weekly and monthly parts from October 17, 1868, to May
22, 1869, and as a book about May 13, 1869.

Set in London, Exeter, "Nuncombe Putney" (Devonshire), and Tuscany.

1868 *The Vicar of Bullhampton* (novel in one volume; ca. 205,000 words).
Written June 15–November 1, 1868. Publishing agreement dated February 1, 1868; published in monthly parts from July, 1869, to May, 1870, and as a book about April 9, 1870.

Set in "Bullhampton" (near Salisbury) and "Loring" (in Gloucestershire).

1868–69 *Sir Harry Hotspur of Humblethwaite* (novel in one volume; ca. 69,000 words).
Written December 27, 1868 to January 30, 1869. Publishing agreement dated March 8, 1869; published serially each month, May–December, 1870, and as a book about November 10 (with date "1871").

Set in Cumberland.

Most of the information about publishing agreements and writing schedules is drawn from Trollope's own records, procured by Michael Sadleir from Henry Trollope for the Bodleian Library, Oxford (MSS. Don. c. 9, 10, and 10*). Publication dates are based on advertisements and announcements in contemporary literary periodicals or in the *Times*. Information about form of publication comes from Michael Sadleir, *Trollope, a Bibliography* (London, 1928; reprinted William Dawson & Sons, 1977), corrected where necessary.

Notes

All Trollope's letters here cited, and some parts of his official reports, will be found under their dates in the collection of his correspondence edited by N. John Hall, forthcoming from the Stanford University Press. Many of them have already been published in Bradford A. Booth, ed., *The Letters of Anthony Trollope* (London: Oxford University Press, 1951).

1. Trollope was at Harrow school from the summer of 1823 to early 1825, then a pupil at a private school conducted by Arthur Jackson Drury at Sunbury, Middlesex; he was a scholar at Winchester from April 14, 1827, to the middle of 1830, then returned to Harrow, from which he withdrew in March, 1834.—MS records at Harrow and Winchester; F. E. Trollope, *Frances Trollope* (London, 1895), 1:94–95; Anthony Trollope, *An Autobiography*, ed. F. Page (London: Oxford University Press, 1950), pp. 5, 26, 29–30. William Drury, Arthur's brother, had been an assistant master at Harrow during Trollope's earlier sojourn there and was currently chaplain of the English Chapel at Brussels.

2. F. Trollope, *Frances Trollope*, 1:225–26; Post Office Records, English Minutes, Post 35, vol. 20, nos. 313V, 400V; Appointments Book, Post 58, vol. 68, no. 558; Establishment Book, Post 59, vol. 37, under "Secretary's Office." See Michael Sadleir, *Trollope, a Commentary* (London: Constable, 1927), p. 111. The publisher John Murray and the physician Henry Holland (later Sir Henry) laid claim to having helped secure the appointment from Freeling.—Samuel Smiles, *A Publisher and His Friends* (London, 1891), 2:384, and T. H. S. Escott,

Anthony Trollope (London, 1913), p. 18. The probationary period was three months: House of Commons, *Sessional Papers*, 1849, vol. 23:116.

3. *Autobiography*, pp. 35–37; *Daily News* (London), January 5, 1861, p. 5, col. 5.

4. Post Office Records, Establishment Books, Post 59, vols. 36, 40, 42, under "Secretary's Office"; House of Commons, *Sessional Papers*, 1835, vol. 48:358.

5. In 1855 Trollope said that of the eight junior clerks who served in the office about 1835, two had been dismissed, one had died, and the other five were still in the service at salaries ranging from £500 to £900 per annum.—Trollope, "The Civil Service," *Dublin University Magazine* 46 (October, 1855):423.

6. *Dictionary of National Biography*, s.v. "Freeling," "Maberly"; Edmund Yates, *Recollections and Experiences* (London, 1884), 1:96–99. Maberly died February 6, 1885, aged nearly eighty-seven.

7. Post Office Records, uncataloged, in boxes of "Secretary's Orders."

8. Professor Bradford Booth claimed to have found in the Post Office records in 1947 or 1948 a memorandum opposite Trollope's name, in the handwriting of the secretary: "A very bad clerk." I have not seen such a memorandum.—*Barchester Towers*, ed. Booth (New York: Rinehart, 1949), p. viii.

9. Post Office Records, English Minutes, Post 35, vol. 27, no. 562CC; vol. 30, nos. 301EE and 470EE; "Secretary's Orders."

10. *Dublin University Magazine* 46:421. Trollope uses this anecdote in chap. 35 of *Marion Fay*.

11. Post Office Records, Irish Minutes, Post 36, vol. 12, no. 1002; English Minutes, Post 35, vol. 47, no. 400.

12. Pp. 46–47.

13. *The Life of Cicero* (London, 1880), 1:195–96.

14. T. A. Trollope, *What I Remember* (London, 1887), 1:249–50; *Phineas Finn*, chap. 3.

15. *Autobiography*, pp. 43–46, 50–57; F. Trollope, *Frances Trollope*, 1:216, 220; *Phineas Redux*, chaps. 56, 64; Smiles, *A Publisher and His Friends*, 2:384. For Anthony's

strenuous reading plans at this time, see N. John Hall, "An Unpublished Trollope Manuscript on a Proposed History of World Literature" and "Trollope's Commonplace Book, 1835–40," *Nineteenth-Century Fiction* 29 (September, 1974):206–10; 31 (June, 1976):15–25.

16. "The Civil Service," *Fortnightly Review* 2 (October 15, 1865):623.

17. *Autobiography*, p. 50; F. Trollope, *Frances Trollope*, 1:259, 299–300, 306; T. A. Trollope, *What I Remember*, 1:359, 370, 374; Sadleir, *Commentary*, pp. 124–25; Post Office Records, English Minutes, Post 35, vol. 35, no. 1044JJ and vol. 36, nos. 260KK, 442KK, 1025KK. The York Street address is confirmed in the register of the marriage of Cecilia Trollope to John Tilley, St. Mary's Church, Bryanston Square, February 11, 1839 (now housed in the Marylebone Public Library, Marylebone Road). See also Trollope's letter to Tilley, April 7, 1849.

18. Post Office Records, Establishment Book, Post 59, vol. 42; marriage register as above. The Post Office colleague in the party was J. H. Newman.

19. *Autobiography*, pp. 57–59; Post Office Records, English Minutes, Post 35, vol. 42, no. 651QQ. Stephen Maberly was a surveyor's clerk in Ireland from 1839, Edward Maberly and Livesay Maberly from 1846.—Establishment Books, Post 59, vols. 43, 45. Trollope's predecessor as surveyor's clerk, George L. Turner, was not in fact dismissed as *An Autobiography* suggests, but transferred to the Money Order Office in Dublin.—Salary Book, Post 58, vol. 64, end.

20. Post Office Records, English Minutes, Post 35, vol. 43, nos. 78RR, 174RR, 273RR. Adolphus Edward Shelley (1812–54) was third son of Sir John Shelley, 6th Bart.

21. *Autobiography*, pp. 61–63; Trollope's MS Travel Accounts, Parrish Collection, Princeton University, vol. 1. The secretary of the Post Office in Ireland was Augustus Godby.

22. *Autobiography*, pp. 58–59; Post Office Records, Establishment Books, Post 59, vols. 40, 44 (Ireland); letter of December 25, 1858, to B. Blake. There are six volumes of traveling accounts and journals (September 15,

1841–September 18, 1871) in the Princeton University Library. On their testimony, Trollope's gross income for the first twelve months in Ireland was £406.8.1, but his income after expenses was £313.4.2 (or, correcting for his faulty addition, £314.4.2).

23. *An Autobiography* does not specify which postmaster Trollope was dealing with, and the dismissal of Irish postmasters for arrearage was very common. Oranmore was in Trollope's district, "in the far west of county Galway," and records show that the postmaster there was dismissed at this time.—Post Office Records, Irish Minutes, Post 36, vol. 12, nos. 952, 1026, 1053, 1063; *Autobiography*, pp. 65–66. Trollope's traveling journals show him at Headford, twenty-three miles from Oranmore, on October 1, 6–13, 1841.

24. Post Office Records, Irish Minutes, Post 36, vol. 12, nos. 1002, 1017.

25. *Autobiography*, pp. 63–64.

26. Trollope's traveling journals, 1842, and Post Office Records, Irish Minutes, Post 36, vol. 13, no. 955. Thomas Bland was appointed to the Inland Office on December 18, 1841, and transferred to Ireland as surveyor's clerk on September 9, 1844. In 1851 he went to England as a surveyor's clerk and left the service in 1854 or 1855— Salary Book, Post 58, vol. 64 end; Establishment Books, Post 59, vols. 44, 45, 48, 49, 50, 51, 56. I have not established a relationship between him and Joseph Bland.

27. William White, *General Directory of . . . Sheffield, with Rotherham, Chesterfield, [&c.]* (Sheffield, 1845), pp. 337–42, 346, and s.v. "Heseltine"; *Reminiscences of Rotherham & District in the Early Part of the Present Century,* by Local Contributors, reprinted from the "Rotherham Advertiser" (Rotherham, 1891), pp. 118–19, 8–9 (written by John Hague, Heseltine's former clerk), 38. For Heseltine's collection of armor, see the *Sheffield and Rotherham Independent,* February 22, 1851, p. 8, col. 5. Heseltine had an unfortunate end: when he retired from the bank at the end of 1853, it was discovered that there were serious irregularities in the books. Heseltine, who had moved to

the coast for his health, was never publicly called to account and the defalcation was not made public. But the fear of prosecution led him to move to Le Havre in February, 1855, and there he died seven months later, on September 15.—"Mr. Trollope's Father-in-Law," *The Three Banks Review*, no. 66 (June, 1965), pp. 25–38. (I am indebted to Professor N. John Hall for the reference, which the late Lord Snow had used in his *Trollope* [London, 1975], p. 60, but never identified.)

28. *Doctor Thorne*, chap. 7.
29. *Autobiography*, pp. 68, 71; Post Office Records, "Promotion Class to Class," Post 30/164 Eng 3849/1863 (official letter to John Tilley, May 24, 1863); *Sheffield and Rotherham Independent*, June 15, 1844, p. 5, col. 6. Rose Trollope's memoranda are in the library of the University of Illinois, Urbana-Champaign; they and the traveling journals indicate his movements.
30. *Autobiography*, pp. 70–71; Bodleian Library, Oxford, MS. Don. c. 9, fols. 1–6; List of New Books, *Athenaeum*, April 3, 1847, p. 364. Trollope's traveling journals put him at Drumsna from August 23, 1843, and he has written crosswise opposite the entries for September 13–24, "Began my first novel."
31. Post Office Records, Irish Minutes, Post 36, vol. 16, nos. 864, 893, 943; English Minutes, Post 35, vol. 60, no. 3771. Bland is described as being at that moment on a visit to friends in Westmorland (the Tilleys?).
32. Family records now in the Library of the University of Illinois.
33. Post Office Records, Irish Minutes, Post 36, vol. 25, nos. 272, 291, 350a; Rose Trollope's MS memoranda, University of Illinois; *Autobiography*, pp. 96–97.
34. Post Office Records, Irish Minutes, Post 36, vol. 27, nos. 2311, 105.
35. T. A. Trollope, *What I Remember*, 1:258–59.
36. Trollope later remarked, "The descent from O'Connell to Mr. Butt has been the natural declension of a political disease, which we had no right to hope would be cured by any one remedy."—*Autobiography*, p. 73. Professor N. John Hall has supplied me with the newspaper accounts

of Trollope's appearances as witness in the case, at a first trial in late March that ended when a juror became ill, and at the second trial on July 26 that ended with a hung jury.—*Tralee Chronicle*, Saturday, March 31, 1849, and *Kerry Evening Post*, July 28, 1849. Justin McCarthy, who was present in the courtroom in July, gives a somewhat fictionalized account of how Trollope followed the marked coin from post office to post office until, when it disappeared, he seized the guilty postmistress; in fact, Trollope was too well known to postmasters and postmistresses to have followed the letter incognito. O'Reilly even knew something was up when she heard that Trollope was unexpectedly at Ardfert on the fatal day, but it was too late.—McCarthy, *Reminiscences* (New York, 1899), 1:369–72.

37. *Autobiography*, pp. 83–84, 86–87; Helen G. King, "Trollope's Letters to the *Examiner*," *Princeton University Library Chronicle* 26 (Winter, 1965):71–101.

38. Post Office Records, Establishment Book, Post 59, vol. 45, "Secretary's Office"; Sir Rowland Hill's Post Office Journals (MS), Post 100, passim.

39. Trollope, *Thackeray* (London, 1879), p. 34; Gordon N. Ray, ed., *The Letters and Private Papers of William Makepeace Thackeray* (Cambridge, Mass.: Harvard University Press, 1946), 2:427–28, 431–33 (Thackeray to Lady Blessington, September–October 1, 1848).

40. House of Commons, *Sessional Papers*, 1854–55, vol. 11:307; *Autobiography*, pp. 87–92.

41. Post Office Records, Rowland Hill Papers, Post 100, vol. 37, nos. 1236a, 1251; Irish Minutes, Post 36, vol. 33, no. 2273 and vol. 35, no. 1233; Trollope's traveling journal, vol. 3.

42. Post Office Records, Rural Posts, Post 14, vol. 28, nos. 1189, 1345, 1470, 1472, 1474, 1734, 1830, 1844, 2004, 2035. Trollope's long letter on Dawlish and Teignmouth, dated "Exeter 27 October 1851," together with his detailed returns on his proposals, is Post 14, vol. 40, no. 1706.

43. Post Office Records, Rural Posts, Post 14, vol. 28, no. 1206; *Autobiography*, pp. 88–91. I do not know how Trollope arrived at his figure of twopence-farthing a

day for his postmistress's stipend in *Small House* (below). That would amount to one shilling, three pence, three farthings for a seven-day week, or about three pounds, eight shillings, five pence a year. Rural messengers, who walked sixteen miles a day on their delivery routes, were paid twelve to fourteen shillings a week, town supplementary letter carriers about half that amount, a rural subpostmaster about twelve shillings, and the postmaster in a country town £40 to £50 a year.

44. Post Office Records, Hill's (MS) Post Office Journals, Post 100, vol. 11, pp. 432–33, 435. At this point Hill believed that Maberly was "much annoyed at Tilley's having become an earnest P.O. reformer [i.e., a partisan of Hill], and [desired] to cause ill-will between us. The other day he said to Tilley 'When I'm gone, you'll go to the work-house. Hill will get rid of you somehow or other.' " Trollope addressed a letter to Lord Hardwicke, the postmaster general, on November 25, applying for the Mail Coach position (British Library), and Tilley called on Hardwicke at home to ask for Trollope's appointment.

45. *Autobiography*, p. 97; letter of November 27, 1852; Escott, *Anthony Trollope*, pp. 113, 115.

46. Trollope's traveling journal, vol. 3; Post Office Records, Post 30, File No. E685 K/1814, Folders 49 B, F. Letters (reports) from Trollope are dated November 21, 1851 (one letter only, not, as Booth's edition says, two) and January 25, 1853.

47. Post Office Records, Post 30, File No. E685 K/1814, Folders 49 B, F.

48. For example, "Second Report of the Postmaster General," House of Commons, *Sessional Papers*, 1856, vol. 37:71.

49. Post Office Records, Wall Letter Boxes, Post 30/212, E9586/1871. Memoranda by Trollope are dated February 5, February 23, May 24, and July 4, 1861.

50. Post Office Records, Tilley's Private Letter Books, Post 101, vol. 8, pp. 13–14.

51. *Autobiography*, pp. 92–93, 95. Trollope's travel diaries show that he was in and about Salisbury in late May, 1852, and that he was in Tenbury on Friday, July 29,

1853. The Page edition of *An Autobiography,* following Trollope's manuscript rather than the posthumous first edition, gives the latter date as July 29, 1852, and by presumption makes the former date 1851. But the manuscript is erroneous and the first edition, seen through the press by Trollope's older son Henry, is here correct with its "1853."

52. Post Office Records, Irish Minutes, Post 36, vol. 36, no. 998; vol. 37, nos. 1273, 1635; vol. 38, nos. 604–5; vol. 40, nos. 40, 69; English Minutes, Post 35, vol. 137, no. 6123; Trollope's traveling journal, vol. 3.

53. Post Office Records, Irish Minutes, Post 36, vol. 40, no. 297; Tilley's Private Letter Books, Post 101, vol. 2, pp. 166, 168, 174–75, 183; Irish Minutes, Post 36, vol. 41, nos. 841, 846, 850, 899; "Report from the Select Committee on Postal Arrangements (Waterford, &c)," House of Commons, *Sessional Papers,* 1854–55, vol. 11:431–532. Trollope was in London from June 26 to August 2, 1855. "I have travelled all over Ireland, closely as few other men can have done," he boasted at the beginning of *Castle Richmond.*

54. Rose Trollope's MS memoranda, University of Illinois; illustration in *Autobiography,* facing p. 65.

55. Post Office Records, Establishment Books, Post 59, vols. 53, 56; *Autobiography,* pp. 102–3.

56. "The Civil Service," *Dublin University Magazine* 46 (October, 1855):410. Trollope was paid eight guineas for this article.

57. P. 413. See also *The Three Clerks* (1858), 2: chap. 12 ("The Civil Service"). *The Bertrams* (1859) begins with strong condemnation of the moral effects of competitive examinations for the youth.

58. "Report of the Select Committee on Civil Service Appointments," House of Commons, *Sessional Papers,* 1860, vol. 9:174–75. The commission looked into Trollope's charges and found that they had been asked to examine the candidates for a *clerkship;* they would certainly have passed Trollope's man for a sorter.—*Sessional Papers,* 1861, vol. 19:532–33. See Post Office Records, Tilley's Private Letter Books, Post 101, vol. 5, pp. 29, 58–59,

212, 215, and English Minutes, Post 35, vol. 203, no. 1600. For the sore throat, see Bodleian, MS. Don. c. 9, fol. 72.

59. "Third Report of the Postmaster General on the Post Office," House of Commons, *Sessional Papers*, 1857:1, vol. 4:354–61.

60. Post Office Records, Tilley's Private Letter Books, Post 101, vol. 4, pp. 57, 60; Trollope's traveling journal, vol. 4; letter to Rose Trollope, Paris, January 31, 1858.

61. Post Office Records, "Substitution of bags for iron boxes in transmission of mails for Australia," Post 29/126 Packet 256R/1866. Trollope's reports are dated from Alexandria on February 14 and April 3, 1858; from Malta on April 16; and from London on May 22.

62. Post Office Records, "Indian Mail Service. Conveyance through Egypt," Post 29/86 Packet 1004I/1858. Trollope's reports are dated from Cairo, February 16, from Suez, February 23, from Alexandria, March 25, from Glasgow, June 19, and from Dublin, July 1, 1858. See his account in *Autobiography*, pp. 116, 118, 122–25. Dates of his movements are in his traveling journal. The commendation is House of Commons, *Sessional Papers*, 1859:1, vol. 8:448. Nubar Bey, a newcomer on the Egyptian scene, was an Armenian Christian who rose to the premiership of Egypt in the latter part of the century.

63. Post Office Records, "Malta—Extension of Money Order System to," Post 29/102 Packet 860M/1861. Trollope's report is dated from Malta, April 16, 1858, and amended by him in London on May 18. He has also drawn up a schedule of the incomes of the Malta Post Office employees, dated April 15. He wrote a comment, dated September 28, on a letter sent to London by the deputy postmaster general at Malta. For *Doctor Thorne* and *The Bertrams* see *Autobiography*, pp. 117–18, 122.

64. Rose Trollope's MS memoranda, University of Illinois; Post Office Records, Irish Minutes, Post 36, vol. 48, no. 768; *Autobiography*, pp. 127–28.

65. Trollope's instructions are in Post Office Records, "Instructions to Packet Agents, Colonial Postmasters, &c." Post 44, vol. 12, pp. 95–101; also Tilley's Private Letter

Books, Post 101, vol. 4, pp. 142, 153; *The West Indies and the Spanish Main*, p. 7.

66. *West Indies*, p. 8; Post Office Records, "Transfer of Post Office Control to the local Authorities in Jamaica, &c." Post 29/96 Packet 531L/1860. Trollope's official letters are dated from Kingston, December 25, 1858, and January 22, 1859; another, February 3, 1859, includes memoranda made in Jamaica on December 28 and January 18.

67. Post Office Records, "West Indies. Next Routes for Mail Services," Post 29/93 Packet 204L/1860 (items 17–19 of Trollope's report of July 16, 1859).

68. *West Indies*, chaps. 11–14; letter of instructions dated November 16, 1858, items 10, 12.

69. Letter of instructions dated November 16, 1858, item 17; Post Office Records, "Grenada Postal Convention for the Isthmus of Panama," Post 29/102 Packet 1105M/1861. Trollope's reports are dated from Panama on May 8 and London on July 25, 1859.

70. *West Indies*, pp. 256–58, 334, 338, 345–46, 155.

71. Muriel R. Trollope, "What I Was Told," *The Trollopian* 2 (March, 1948):232; *West Indies*, pp. 275–76; Gordon N. Ray, *Thackeray, The Age of Wisdom* (New York: McGraw Hill, 1958), p. 215; Trollope, *Thackeray*, p. 60; Trollope's letter to Herman Merivale, January 13, 1864.

72. *West Indies*, pp. 367, 388–95; *Times* (London), July 5, 1859, p. 12, col. 5.

73. *West Indies*, p. 2; Post Office Records, "West Indies. Next Routes for Mail Services," Post 29/93 Packet 204L/1860 (Trollope's letters and reports are dated from London on July 16 and two on September 6); House of Commons, *Sessional Papers*, 1860, vol. 23:337–38; *Autobiography*, p. 125.

74. Rose Trollope's MS memoranda, University of Illinois; letters to B. Blake, July 10, and Rose Trollope, August 2, 1859; Post Office Records, Tilley's Private Letter Books, Post 101, vol. 4, pp. 275, 282; English Minutes, Post 35, vol. 192, no. 3794; vol. 196, no. 123; "Surveyors' Districts Rearrangement," Post 30/172 E1913/1866; *Autobiography*, pp. 132–33, 147. The farmhouse of

Orley Farm is of course pictured from the comfortable farmhouse of Julians Hill at Harrow, in which Trollope lived as a boy, but it is transplanted from Middlesex to one of the eastern counties.

75. Post Office Records, English Minutes, Post 35, vol. 201, nos. 818, 833; vol. 202, no. 1025; vol. 239, no. 1173; vol. 251, nos. 1680, 1693, 1981; vol. 252, nos. 2181, 2360, 2536; vol. 241, nos. 2641, 3224.

76. Letters of June 1, 1862; May 24, 1863; June 15, 1863; September 30, 1863; October 10, 1862; November 22, 1863.

77. Letters to Merivale, ca. December 1860 and December 7, 1860; Royal Literary Fund, Minutes of the General Committee, February 28 and March 14, 1866; *Autobiography and Letters of Charles Merivale*, ed. Judith Anne Merivale (Oxford: Privately Printed, 1898), p. 331.

78. This and the next three paragraphs are drawn from Post Office Records, "Committee of Enquiry into Inadequate Payment of Staff & Lack of Accommodation for the Circulation Department," Post 30/148 4801/1861. The confidential printed report with its substantial minutes of evidence before the committee is in this file. See also English Minutes, Post 35, vol. 203, nos. 1716*, 1868.

79. Post Office Records, Hill's Post Office Journals, Post 100, vol. 14, pp. 2–3 and passim, January–June 1861.

80. "Mr. Anthony Trollope on the Civil Service," *Daily News* (London), January 5, 1861, p. 5, col. 6.

81. Post Office Records, Hill's Post Office Journals, Post 100, vol. 14, pp. 2–3; vol. 15, p. 66.

82. Post Office Records, Tilley's Private Letter Books, Post 101, vol. 5, pp. 29, 58–59, 74, 77; "Report of the Select Committee on Civil Service Appointments," House of Commons, *Sessional Papers*, 1860, vol. 9:158–80; Post Office Records, "Promotion Class to Class," Post 30/164 Eng 3849/1863.

83. *Times* (London), December 1, 1883, p. 7, col. 6; Post Office Records, Hill's Post Office Journals, Post 100, vol. 17, pp. 174–75; *Autobiography*, p. 133.

84. Yates, *Recollections*, 2:232.

85. Bodleian, MS. Don. c. 10*, fols. 87–88.

86. Bodleian, MSS. Don. c. 9, fols. 82–83; Don. c. 10*, fols. 99–100.

87. An early writing calendar for *Brown, Jones, and Robinson* is slipped into Trollope's traveling journal, vol. 4; he wrote thirty-two pages of manuscript (about 8,000 words) between August 24 and September 7, 1857. "The Civil Service as a Profession," *Cornhill Magazine* 3 (February, 1861):215–17; T. A. Trollope to Anthony Trollope, Florence, July 27, 1860 (MS in University of Illinois Library).

88. Bodleian, MS. Don. c. 9, fols. 89–90.

89. Post Office Records, English Minutes, Post 35, vol. 212, no. 1682.

90. Post Office Records, English Minutes, Post 35, vol. 212, no. 1877; Hill's Post Office Journals, Post 100, vol. 15, pp. 66, 50, 52, 57; *Autobiography*, pp. 162–63; *Athenaeum*, no. 1819 (September 6, 1862), p. 306; Rowland Hill and G. B. Hill, *The Life of Sir Rowland Hill* (London, 1880), 2:361–62.

91. Trollope, *North America*, ed. Donald Smalley and Bradford A. Booth (New York: Alfred A. Knopf, 1951), pp. 164–65, 312–14, 465–79.

92. "Tenth Report of the Postmaster General," House of Commons, *Sessional Papers*, 1864, vol. 30:614; Post Office Records, English Minutes, Post 35, vol. 232, nos. 1286, 1339; Establishment Book, Post 59, vol. 56.

93. Post Office Records, English Minutes, Post 35, vol. 143, no. 2497; vol. 191, no. 3181.

94. Post Office Records, Minuted Papers, Post 30/185 E3174/1868; English Minutes, Post 35, vol. 232, no. 1846.

95. Post Office Records, Minuted Papers, Post 30/185 E3174/1868.

96. Post Office Records, Tilley's Private Letter Books, Post 101, vol. 6, p. 184; Minuted Papers, Post 30/185 E3174/1868.

97. *Autobiography*, p. 134; Barry A. Bartrum, "A Victorian Political Hostess: The Engagement Book of Lady Stanley of Alderley," *Princeton University Library Chronicle* 36 (Winter, 1975):133–46.

98. Fragment of letter to an unidentified correspondent, July 27, 1864 (MS in Parrish Collection, Princeton University).

99. This affirmation is based on the Post Office records, but Trollope himself also made it in *An Autobiography*, p. 163n, where the pain of the present dispute shows through, though he never mentions it: "During the period of my service in the Post Office I did very much special work for which I never asked any remuneration,—and never received any, though payments for special services were common in the department at that time."

100. Post Office Records, Tilley's Private Letter Books, Post 101, vol. 6, pp. 270, 274, 278; vol. 8, p. 135.

101. Post Office Records, Hill's Post Office Journals, Post 100, vol. 17, p. 170.

102. Post Office Records, "Committee of Enquiry into Inadequate Payment of Staff & Lack of Accommodation," Post 30/148 4801/1861.

103. Post Office Records, English Minutes, Post 35, vol. 251, nos. 1619, 1952.

104. Post Office Records, English Minutes, Post 35, vol. 252, nos. 2498, 2796, 2892; vol. 253, no. 3239; Tilley's Private Letter Books, Post 101, vol. 8, pp. 133–35, 137; vol. 9, p. 141.

105. Post Office Records, English Minutes, Post 35, vol. 253, nos. 3242, 3282; vol. 254, no. 4041; Tilley's Private Letter Books, Post 101, vol. 8, pp. 148, 154. There is a printed schedule of salaries dated February 15, 1867, in the bundle of documents on the Reorganization of the London Post Office, Post 30/184 E2987/1868.

106. Yates, *Recollections*, 2:230–31.

107. Post Office Records, "Surveyors' Districts Rearrangement," Post 30/172 E1913/1866.

108. Post Office Records, English Minutes, Post 35, vol. 263, no. 4208 and vol. 222, no. 3113; Tilley's Private Letter Books, Post 101, vol. 9, pp. 163, 176; *Autobiography*, pp. 277–81; Bodleian, MS. Don. c. 10*, fols. 7–8 (Trollope to James Virtue, December 14, 1866); Escott, *Anthony Trollope*, p. 257, taken in conjunction with the figure

mentioned by Sadleir, *Commentary*, p. 272, and Trollope's entry at the end of his travel diary for 1868:
"Editing St Pauls £750." Tilley's formal official letter is
in the Parrish Collection, Princeton University. The
concluding sentence of the paragraph is based on a
photostat in the Post Office Records of a memorandum
in Trollope's hand dated October 10, 1867; I have not
seen the original.

109. *World*, no. 921, (February 24, 1892):19.

110. *Times* (London), November 2, 1867, p. 9, col. 6; *Spectator*
40 (November 2, 1867):1219.

111. Letter of April 18, 1878; *Who Was Who, 1897–1916;*
obituary in *Times* (London), March 19, 1898, p. 7, col. 6.

112. "Fourteenth Report of the Postmaster General," House
of Commons, *Sessional Papers*, 1867–68, vol. 22:733–34;
"Postal Conventions (England and America)," *Sessional
Papers*, 1868–69, vol. 34:437, 441, etc.; "Report from
the Select Committee on Mail Contracts," *Sessional
Papers*, 1868–69, vol. 6:363, 376–77; Post Office Records, Minuted Documents, Post 29/152 Packet 949T/
1868. Trollope's letters are dated from Waltham Cross,
February 29, 1868; from Washington, May 1, May 18
(also a formal report on this date), May 26, July 3 (on
this date a telegram, two letters, and three sheets of
memoranda), July 7, July 11 (a telegram), July 12. His
statement of expenses is dated at the General Post Office, July 27, and there is a printed copy of the 1867
agreement with amendments in Trollope's hand, initialed by Randall on July 11.

113. Post Office Records, Tilley's Private Letter Books, Post
101, vol. 10, p. 8; vol. 9, pp. 174–75 for F. Hill's eco-
nomic doctrine. For the levee, *Times*, March 18, 1868, p.
5, col. 3.

114. Tilley's Private Letter Books, Post 101, vol. 10, pp. 124,
134.

115. Letters to Kate Field, June 3 and 10, 1868; *South Africa*
(1878), 1:121.

116. Letter to Kate Field, July 13, 1868.

117. Letter to Kate Field, July 8, 1868.

118. *Autobiography*, p. 308.

119. He protested vigorously against the deprivation, for example in "The Civil Service as a Profession," *Cornhill Magazine* 3 (February, 1861):227–28.
120. Letter from Trollope to Anna C. Steele, November 21, 1868 (misdated 1869 in Booth's edition).
121. House of Commons, *Sessional Papers*, 1868–69, vol. 50:13, 109.
122. Detailed accounts of the election, drawn from newspapers and local archives, are given by Lance O. Tingay, "Trollope and the Beverley Election." *Nineteenth-Century Fiction* 5 (June, 1950):23–37; Arthur Pollard, *Trollope's Political Novels* (Hull: University of Hull, 1968), pp. 3–13 and frontispiece; and John Halperin, *Trollope and Politics* (London: Macmillan, 1977), pp. 112–26. See also facsimiles in *Autobiography*, pp. 303–4.
123. "In and Out of Society," *Life* (London) 5 (December 14, 1882):1037. I have not been able to establish the date for this appearance.
124. "Minutes of the Evidence taken at the Trial of the Beverley Election Petition," House of Commons, *Sessional Papers*, 1868–69, vol. 48:415–523.
125. House of Commons, *Sessional Papers*, 1870, all of vol. 39; vol. 56: 175, 177; vol. 1:165–69.
126. House of Commons, *Sessional Papers*, 1870, vol. 29:250–51; 1868–69, vol. 50:13, 60.
127. "It had seemed to me that nothing could be worse, nothing more unpatriotic, nothing more absolutely opposed to the system of representative government, than the time-honoured practices of the borough of Beverley. It had come to pass that political cleanliness was odious to the citizens. . . . To have assisted in putting an end to this, even in one town, was to a certain extent a satisfaction."—*Autobiography*, p. 306; see also pp. 298–300. Two of Trollope's electioneering characters received the same warning he said had been given to him. Sir Thomas Underwood was told at Percycross, "You'll spend a thousand pounds in the election. You won't get in, of course, but you'll petition. That'll be another thousand. You'll succeed there, and disfranchise the borough. It will be a great career, and no doubt you'll find

it satisfactory. You mustn't show yourself in Percycross afterwards;—that's all."—*Ralph the Heir,* chap. 20. And Phineas Finn was told at Tankerville in Durham, "There isn't a borough in England more sure to return a Liberal than Tankerville if left to itself. And yet that lump of a legislator has sat there as a Tory for the last dozen years by dint of money and brass. . . . He will be elected. You'll petition. He'll lose his seat. There will be a commission. And then the borough will be disfranchised. It's a fine career, but expensive; and then there is no reward beyond the self-satisfaction arising from a good action."—*Phineas Redux,* chap. 1.

128. Letter to Anna C. Steele, November 21, 1868.

129. T. A. Trollope, *What I Remember,* 2:127–29.

130. *Life of Cicero,* 1:130. "Perhaps nothing more disagreeable, more squalid, more revolting to the senses, more opposed to personal dignity, [than Parliamentary canvassing] can be conceived. . . . But to go through it and then not to become a member is base indeed!"—*The Duke's Children,* chap. 55.

131. Post Office Records, Tilley's Private Letter Books, Post 101, vol. 9, p. 176; Trollope to Tom Taylor, April 10, 1874.

132. *South Africa,* 1:77; *How the "Mastiffs" Went to Iceland,* p. 14.

133. *John Caldigate,* chaps. 52, 64. My friend in the research room of the Post Office Records Department thus explained these alphabetical phenomena: the so-called check letters indicated the position of each stamp on the engraved sheet of 240 stamps. The top row of stamps would be lettered A-A, A-B, A-C, etc., to A-L, the second row B-A, B-B, B-C, etc., to B-L, for twenty horizontal rows and twelve vertical columns, i.e., to T-J, T-K, T-L.—J. B. Seymour, *The Stamps of Great Britain,* pt. 1 (London: Royal Philatelic Society, 1934), pp. 31–32. What Bagwax must have learned was that in 1874 the number of vertical columns of stamps on a sheet was increased at least to sixteen (letter P): I cannot find that this is true. Moreover, stamps from New South Wales do not show the corner letters in question.

134. *Good Words* 18 (June, 1877):377–84, and 19 (January, 1878):1–19; letter from Trollope to Donald Macleod, January 23, 1877.

135. "Any acceleration—even five minutes—in the arrival of the limited Mail at Glasgow is entirely out of the question," Tilley wrote to an impatient Trollope in Glasgow.—Post Office Records, Tilley's Private Letter Books, Post 101, vol. 8, p. 14 (May 27, 1865). Every printed text of *Phineas,* including that in Trollope's *St. Pauls Magazine,* reads "reached London by some day-mail from Glasgow." The manuscript, in the Beinecke Rare Book and Manuscript Library at Yale University, clearly has no hyphen. Whether the word is "same," as I believe the sense requires, or "some," as printed, cannot be confidently determined from Trollope's handwriting.

136. Dickens's remarks in *Little Dorrit* were of course an echo of Carlyle, and Trollope had a word or two about Carlyle's criticism of government "red tape" in *The Warden,* chap. 15.

137. This observation is hardly new: Mr. and Mrs. Gerould make it in their *Guide to Trollope* (Princeton: Princeton University Press, 1948), s.v. "London."

138. The distant cousin was the Rev. Arthur William Trollope (1768–1827), vicar of Harting from 1792 to 1797.

Index